SCOTT FORESMAN · ADDISON WESLEY

Mathematics

Grade 5

Every
Student
Learns

With a Foreword by Dr. Jim Cummins

ESL Consultant
Darrel Nickolaisen
Teacher/Consultant
Apple Valley, California

PEARSON
Scott
Foresman

Editorial Offices: Glenview, Illinois • Parsippany, New Jersey • New York, New York

Sales Offices: Parsippany, New Jersey • Duluth, Georgia • Glenview, Illinois
Coppell, Texas • Ontario, California • Mesa, Arizona

Overview

Every Student Learns is a lesson-by-lesson companion to
Scott Foresman - Addison Wesley Mathematics and Matemáticas Scott
Foresman - Addison Wesley. It has been designed to provide manageable
support for teachers and their students who are challenged by language issues in
Mathematics, no matter what the first language may be.

Every Student Learns is built upon the Three Pillars of English Language Learning
in the Content Areas by Dr. Jim Cummins of the University of Toronto:

- Activate Prior Knowledge/Build Background
- Access Content
- Extend Language

ISBN: 0-328-07554-X

4 5 6 7 8 9 10 V004 09 08 07 06 05

Table of Contents

Supporting ESL Students
in Learning the Language of Mathematics

DR. JIM CUMMINS • UNIVERSITY OF TORONTO

Mathematics and Language

Mathematics can legitimately be considered to be a language in itself in that it employs symbols to represent concepts, symbols that facilitate our thinking about aspects of reality. However, mathematics is also intimately related to the natural language that we begin to acquire as infants, the language we use to communicate in a variety of everyday and academic contexts. Mathematics and language are interconnected at several levels:

- Teachers use natural language to explain mathematical concepts and perform mathematical operations. Students who have limited proficiency in English require additional support in order to understand mathematical concepts and operations taught in English. Among the supports that teachers can use to make instruction comprehensible for English language learners are demonstrations; concrete, hands-on manipulatives and graphic organizers; simplification and paraphrasing of instructional language; and direct teaching of key vocabulary.

- As is the case in other academic disciplines, mathematics uses a specialized technical vocabulary to represent concepts and, in the case of mathematics, describe operations. As early as Grade 1, students are required to learn the meanings of such words as *addition, subtraction, sum,* and *addend,* words that are likely to be found only in mathematics discourse. Furthermore, other terms have specific meanings in mathematics discourse that differ from their meanings in everyday usage and in other subject areas. Examples of these kinds of terms include words such as *table, product, even,* and *odd.* Homophones such as *sum* and *some* may also be confusing for ESL students. Grade 1 students are required to learn key concepts, such as *number facts* and *addition sentences,* at a time when many of them (ESL students, in particular) may not know the broader meanings of words such as *facts* and *sentences.*

- In addition to the technical vocabulary of mathematics, language intersects with mathematics at the broader level of general vocabulary, syntax, semantics, and discourse. Most mathematical problems require students to understand propositions and logical relations that are expressed through language. Consider this problem at the Grade 4 level:

  Wendy gave a total of 10 treats to her dogs. She gave her large dog 2 more treats than she gave her small dog. How many treats did she give to each dog?

  Here students need to understand (or be able to figure out) the meanings of words such as *total* and *treats.* They need to understand the logical relation expressed by the *more ... than ...* construction. And they need to infer that Wendy has only two dogs, even though this fact is not explicitly included in the problem. Clearly, the language demands of the math curriculum increase as students progress through the grades, and these demands can cause particular difficulties for ESL students.

© Pearson Education, Inc., 5

The ESL Challenge

Numerous research studies have demonstrated that ESL students generally require at least 5 years to catch up to native speakers in academic language proficiency (i.e., reading and writing skills; see Cummins, 2001 for a review). In mathematics, ESL students often make good progress in acquiring basic computation skills in the early grades. However, they typically experience greater difficulty in learning to interpret and solve word problems, and this difficulty increases in the later elementary grades as the word problems become more linguistically and conceptually complex.

These developmental patterns can be understood in relation to three very different aspects of language proficiency:

- **Conversational fluency** is the ability to carry on a conversation in familiar face-to-face situations. This is the kind of proficiency that the vast majority of native speakers of English have developed by the time they enter school at age 5. It involves the use of high-frequency words and simple grammatical constructions. ESL students generally develop basic fluency in conversational aspects of English within a year or two of exposure to the language, either within school or in their out-of-school environments.

- **Discrete language skills** reflect specific phonological, lexical, and grammatical knowledge that students can acquire in two ways: (a) as a result of direct instruction and (b) through both formal and informal practice (e.g., reading). Some of these discrete language skills are acquired early in schooling, and some continue to be acquired throughout schooling. The discrete language skills that are acquired early include knowledge of the letters of the alphabet, the sounds represented by individual letters and combinations of letters, and the ability to decode written words and pronounce them appropriately. ESL students can learn these specific language skills at a relatively early stage in their acquisition of English; in fact, these skills can be learned concurrently with their development of basic vocabulary and conversational proficiency.

  In mathematics, these discrete language skills include knowledge of the symbols that represent basic mathematical operations (e.g., + and –), the terms used to refer to these symbols and operations (*add, subtract, plus, minus,* etc.), and the basic technical vocabulary of mathematics. Clearly, the ability to decode written text is also a necessary (but not a sufficient) condition for thinking through and solving word problems expressed in written language.

- **Academic language proficiency** includes knowledge of the less frequent vocabulary of English as well as the ability to interpret and produce increasingly complex written language. As students progress through the grades, they encounter far more low-frequency words (primarily from Greek and Latin sources), complex syntax (e.g., the passive voice), and abstract expressions that are virtually never heard in everyday conversation. Students are required to understand linguistically and conceptually demanding texts in the content areas (e.g., literature, social studies, science, and mathematics) and to use this increasingly sophisticated language in accurate and coherent ways in their own writing.

Acquiring academic language proficiency is challenging for all students. Schools spend at least 12 years trying to extend the conversational language that native-speaking children bring to school into these more complex academic language spheres. It is hardly surprising, therefore, that research has repeatedly shown that ESL students usually require at least 5 years of exposure to academic English in order to catch up to native-speaker norms. In addition to internalizing increasingly complex academic language, ESL students must catch up to a moving target. Every year, native speakers are making large gains in their reading and writing abilities and in their knowledge of vocabulary. In order to catch up to grade norms within 6 years, ESL students must make 15 months' gain in every 10-month school year. By contrast, the typical native-speaking student is expected to make 10 months' gain in a 10-month school year (Collier & Thomas, 1999).

All three aspects of language proficiency are important. However, the three aspects—conversational fluency, discrete language skills, and academic language proficiency—are frequently confused by policy makers and by the media. For example, it is sometimes claimed that children acquire language rapidly and that one year of instructional support is sufficient to enable ESL students to catch up academically. In reality, many ESL students who have acquired fluent conversational skills are still a long way from grade-level performance in academic language proficiency (e.g., in reading comprehension in content areas such as math).

Similarly, the learning of discrete language skills does not generalize automatically to academic language proficiency. ESL (and native-speaking) students who can "read" a mathematical problem fluently may have only a very limited understanding of the words and sentences they can decode.

Thus, ESL students may require extended language support within the classroom in order to continue to make grade-level progress in content areas such as mathematics. Despite the fact that these students have acquired conversational fluency in English, together with basic mathematical vocabulary and computational skills, they may still experience gaps in their knowledge of some of the more sophisticated vocabulary, syntax, and discursive features of mathematical language.

Teaching the Language of Mathematics

From an instructional perspective, the relationship between language and mathematics is both two-way and reciprocal. Mathematical knowledge is developed through language, and language abilities can and should be developed through mathematics instruction. Specifically:

- Because mathematical concepts and operations are embedded in language, the specialized vocabulary of mathematics and the discursive features of mathematical propositions must be taught explicitly if students are to make strong academic progress in mathematics.

- Equally important, however, is the fact that in teaching mathematics, we are also developing and reinforcing students' general academic language proficiency. For example, think about the language learning that will likely occur as the teacher explains the following Grade 1 problem to a group of ESL students.

   Is 3 + 8 greater than 10, equal to 10, or less than 10? Explain.

Students will learn not only the specific meanings of the terms *greater than, equal to,* and l*ess than,* but also synonyms for these terms (e.g., a synonym for *great* is *big,* and the meaning of *greater than* is similar to the meaning of *bigger than*). This particular mathematics problem also presents the teacher an opportunity to teach students the general concept of *comparatives* and the general rule for forming comparatives (e.g., *great, greater, greatest; big, bigger, biggest*). The fact that not all comparatives take exactly these forms can also be taught in relation to *less, lesser, least.* Finally, the meaning of the word explain can be taught (e.g., *describe, tell about, tell why you think so*) and related to its use in other subject areas (e.g., science).

The reciprocal interdependence of language and mathematics becomes apparent, and even obvious, when perusing any mathematics textbook. Much of what students are expected to learn in mathematics is presented in written text. Students are required to read the text in order to develop their understanding of math concepts and their ability to solve math problems. Frequently, students are also required to explain orally or in writing how they solved a particular problem. Obviously, teachers and students will discuss these concepts; but without strong reading skills, students will find it very difficult to acquire, and truly assimilate, lesson content. Without strong writing skills, they will have difficulty demonstrating their knowledge of the concepts and skills that they are often, in fact, acquiring. Thus, effective reading and writing skills are necessary for students to make progress in mathematics, particularly as they move through the elementary grades. By the same token, the teaching of mathematics provides important opportunities for teachers to model academic language in their interactions with students and also to teach features of academic language directly (e.g., reading comprehension strategies, comparative adjectives, and context- or content-specific vocabulary).

Effective academic language instruction for ESL students across the curriculum is built on three fundamental pillars:

- **Activate Prior Knowledge/Build Background**
- **Access Content**
- **Extend Language**

In developing mathematical knowledge through language, and language abilities through mathematics, we can apply these three instructional principles in powerful ways.

Activate Prior Knowledge/Build Background

A. Prior knowledge as the foundation of learning
There is general agreement among cognitive psychologists that we learn by integrating new input into our existing cognitive structures or schemata. Our prior experience provides the foundation for interpreting new information. No learner is a blank slate. In fact, learning can be defined as the process of relating new information to the information we already possess. When we read a mathematical problem, for example, we construct meaning by bringing our prior knowledge of language, of mathematics, and of the world in general to the text. Our prior knowledge enables us to make inferences about the meanings of words and expressions that we may not have encountered before. As our prior knowledge expands through new learning, we are enabled to understand a greater range of mathematical concepts and also the language that expresses those concepts.

Thus, a major rationale for activating students' prior knowledge (or if there is minimal prior knowledge on a particular topic or issue, building it with students), is to make the learning process more efficient. It is important to *activate* students' prior knowledge because students may not explicitly realize what they know about a particular topic or issue; consequently, their prior knowledge may not facilitate learning unless it is brought to an immediate, and conscious, level.

B. Prior knowledge and ESL students

In a classroom that includes second-language learners from diverse backgrounds, prior knowledge about a particular topic may vary widely. Thus, simple transmission of certain information or a given skill will fail to connect with the prior knowledge and previous experience of many students. As a result, the input will be much less comprehensible for these students. Some students may have relevant information in their first language (L1), but not realize that there is any connection with what they are learning in English (L2). In other cases, the algorithms and strategies that students have acquired for carrying out math operations in their countries of origin may differ considerably from the procedures they are now being taught in English. Clearly, these discrepancies can cause confusion for students.

In teaching math to ESL students, it is important that we attempt to connect the instruction both with students' prior experience of learning math and with their prior knowledge of the world in general. In building up our own knowledge of students' educational and cultural backgrounds, we can collaborate with ESL teachers, who may have greater access to this information, and also with community volunteers, who can often provide invaluable insights about students' prior learning and cultural knowledge.

Lois Meyer (2000) has expressed clearly the importance of prior knowledge (familiarity with a given topic) in reducing the cognitive load of instruction for ESL students. She notes that the notion of *cognitive load* refers to the number and complexity of new concepts embedded in a particular lesson or text. This cognitive load depends not only on the text itself but also on the students' prior knowledge of the content.

> If the English learner has little entry knowledge about the subject matter, the cognitive load of the lesson will be heavy, for many concepts will be new and unfamiliar. The student will have little basis from which to generate hypotheses regarding the meanings the teacher is conveying through English.

> If the student's entry knowledge of the topic is considerable, this will lighten the cognitive load. Learners can draw on their knowledge to interpret linguistic and non-linguistic clues in the lesson in order to make educated guesses about the meanings of the teacher's talk and text (2000, p. 229).

Clearly, the cognitive load of many mathematical texts is considerable, particularly as students progress through the grades. Finding out what students know about a particular topic allows the teacher to supply relevant concepts or vocabulary that some or all students may be lacking, but which will be important for understanding the upcoming text or lesson. Building this context permits students to understand more complex language and to pursue more cognitively demanding activities. It lessens the cognitive load of the text and frees up students' brain power.

C. Strategies for Activating Prior Knowledge and Building Background

Three types of prior knowledge are relevant to consider in teaching mathematics: prior knowledge of math; knowledge that has been acquired through direct experiences; and knowledge acquired through secondary sources (e.g. books, videos, etc.). We can use brainstorming, role playing, and simulations, as well as connections to literature and other content areas to activate students' prior knowledge and build relevant background knowledge.

- **Connect to Prior Knowledge of Math** In Grade 1 we might activate students' knowledge of counting as a prelude to teaching them to use *counting on* as a tool for addition. Or at the Grade 4 level, we might activate students' knowledge of basic multiplication facts in order to reinforce the foundation for teaching more complex multiplication operations.

- **Connect to Prior Knowledge of Language** Although mathematics has its own technical language that students must learn, we explain this language, and the associated math operations, using more familiar everyday language. For example, in explaining the concept of *subtraction* we will use high frequency expressions such as *take away from* that are likely to be much more familiar to children. Typically, the meaning of this language will be reinforced through demonstrations involving concrete manipulatives or graphic organizers.

- **Connect to Prior Experiences** We can find out from students what activities they engage in outside of school and link mathematics instruction to those activities (e.g., students who engage in various sports can carry out a variety of operations relevant to those sports, such as calculating, comparing, and contrasting batting averages). We can also be proactive in *creating experiences* for students that will promote mathematical knowledge and skill. For example, we might engage parents as collaborators by having them work with their children in calculating the proportion of weekly food expenditures that the family spends on the various food groups, thereby reinforcing both social studies and math concepts.

- **Use Brainstorming, Role Playing, and Simulation** At a very early age most children develop an intuitive sense of "fairness" and an ability to judge whether goods of various kinds (e.g., toys or treats) have been distributed equally or fairly. We can use brainstorming, role-playing, and simulation to carry out a variety of math activities that tap into students' real-life experiences of equal (or fair) distribution. In the early grades, we would likely use concrete manipulatives to support these activities. In intermediate grades, real or simulated data can be used.

We can also link math to the development of critical thinking by having students carry out projects that go beyond the curriculum in various ways. For example, in a class with many ESL students we might have students brainstorm about the languages they know and how they learned them. On the basis of this brainstorming, they could then develop a questionnaire and carry out a more formal survey of the linguistic make-up of the class (or even the entire school). In analyzing data that reflect their own experiences and identities, students' motivation to explore effective analytic strategies and presentation tools (e.g., graphs and computerized slide shows) is likely to be considerably greater than when the activities are more distant from their experiences and interests.

- **Use Literature and Connections to Content** Relatively few people in North America have ever been in a jungle, but most adults and children can describe the main features of jungles as a result of secondary experiences of various sorts. In the classroom, we can use literature, high-interest expository texts, and other forms of media (e.g., videotapes) both to activate students' prior knowledge of math and also to build background knowledge.

  In some cases, connecting to prior experiences will involve use of stories that have been specifically selected because they contain relevant math content. In other cases, we will connect math concepts and operations to other subject matter across the curriculum. For example, we might link math to a social studies unit on government as we discuss where local and state governments get the funds to operate and as we have students calculate the sales taxes that their families pay for various kinds of purchases.

The essential point here is that the more connections we can make both to students' experiences and interests and to other areas of the curriculum, the more relevance math is likely to assume in students' minds and lives. This, in turn, will result in more powerful learning of math.

An additional consideration in activating ESL Students' prior knowledge is that this process communicates a sense of respect for what students already know and an interest in their cultural backgrounds. This affirmation of students' identities increases students' personal and academic confidence and motivates them to invest their identities more strongly in pursuing academic success.

Access Content

How can teachers make the complex language of mathematics comprehensible for students who are still in the process of learning English? How can students be enabled to take ownership of their learning of math concepts and operations rather than just learn rote procedures? One important strategy has already been noted in the previous section. Activating and building students' background knowledge is an essential part of the process of helping students to participate academically and gain access to meaning. When we activate students' prior knowledge we attempt to modify the "soil" so that the seeds of meaning can take root. However, we can also support or *scaffold* students' learning by modifying the input itself. We provide this scaffolding by embedding the content in a *richly redundant context* wherein there are multiple routes to the mathematical meaning at hand in addition to the language itself.

The following list presents a variety of ways of modifying the presentation of mathematical content to ESL students so that they can more effectively get access to the meaning in any given lesson.

- **Use Demonstration** Teachers can take students through a word problem in math, demonstrating step-by-step procedures and strategies in a clear and explicit manner.

- **Use Manipulatives (and Tools and Technology)** In the early grades manipulatives may include counters and blocks that enable students to carry out a mathematical operation, literally with their hands, and actually see the concrete results of that operation. At more advanced levels, measuring tools such as rulers and protractors and technological

© Pearson Education, Inc., 5

aids such as calculators and computers will be used. The effectiveness of these tools will be enhanced if they are used within the context of a project that students are intrinsically motivated to initiate and complete.

- **Use Small-Group Interactions and Peer Questioning** Working either as a whole class or in heterogeneous groups or pairs, students can engage in real-life or simulated projects that require application of a variety of mathematical skills. Díaz-Rico and Weed (2002) give as an example a project in which students are told that the classroom needs to be re-carpeted. They first estimate the area and then check their estimates with measuring tools. Working in groups, students could also calculate the potential cost of floor coverings using prices for various types of floor coverings obtained from local catalogues or advertisements.

- **Use Pictures, Real Objects, and Graphic Organizers** We commonly hear the expression "A picture is worth a thousand words." There is a lot of truth to this when it comes to teaching academic content. Visuals enable students to "see" the basic concept we are trying to teach much more effectively than if we rely only on words. Once students grasp the concept, they are much more likely to be able to figure out the meanings of the words we use to talk about it. Among the visuals we can use in presenting math content are these: *pictures/photographs, real objects, graphic organizers, drawings on overhead projectors,* and *blackline masters.* Graphic organizers are particularly useful because they can be used not only by teachers to present concepts but also by students to take notes, organize their ideas in logical categories, and summarize the results of group brainstorming on particular issues. Some graphic organizers that are useful for teaching math are *Venn diagrams; pie and bar graphs; K-W-L charts* (What we know, what we want to know, and what we have learned; *T-charts* (e.g., for comparing and contrasting); *Problem and Solution charts; Main Idea and Details charts; Cause and Effect charts; Sequence charts;* and *Time Lines.*

- **Clarify Language (Paraphrase Ideas, Enunciate Clearly, Adjust Speech Rate, and Simplify Sentences)** This category includes a variety of strategies and language-oriented activities that clarify the meanings of new words and concepts. Teachers can modify their language to students by *paraphrasing ideas and by explaining new concepts and words.* They can explain new words by providing synonyms, antonyms, and definitions either in English or in the home language of students, if they know it. Important vocabulary can be repeated and recycled as part of the paraphrasing of ideas. Teachers should speak in a natural rhythm, but enunciate clearly and adjust their speech to a rate that ESL students will find easier to understand. Meaning can also be communicated and/or reinforced through gestures, body language, and demonstrations.

Because of their common roots in Latin and Greek, much of the technical math vocabulary in English has cognates in Romance languages, such as Spanish (e.g., *addition—adición*). Students who know these languages can be encouraged to make these cross-linguistic linkages as a means of reinforcing the concept. Bilingual and English-only dictionaries can also be useful tools for language clarification, particularly for intermediate-grade students.

- **Use Total Physical Response, Gestures, and Pantomime** For beginning ESL Students, *Total Physical Response,* activities wherein students act out commands, can be highly effective. Math calculations can be embedded in the commands that students act out. For example, students can progress from fully acting out the command "Take 5 steps forward and then 2 steps backward" to calculating in their heads that they need take only 3 steps forward to reach the destination. Additionally, the meanings of individual words can be demonstrated through *gestures* and *pantomime.*

- **Give Frequent Feedback and Expand Student Responses** *Giving frequent feedback* means responding positively and naturally to all forms of responses. Teachers can let their students know how they are doing by responding to both their words and their actions. Teachers can also assess their students' understanding by asking them to give examples, or by asking them how they would explain a concept or idea to someone else. *Expanding student responses* often means using polar (either/or) questions with students who are just beginning to produce oral English and "wh" (who, what, when, where, why) questions with students who are more fluent. Teachers can easily, and casually, expand their students' one- and two-word answers into complete sentences ("Yes, a triangle does have three sides") and respond to grammatically incorrect answers by recasting them using standard English syntax (Student: "I gotted 4 tens and 1 one"; Teacher: "That's right, you have 4 tens and 1 one").

Extend Language

A systematic focus on and exploration of language is essential if students are to develop knowledge of the specific vocabulary and discursive patterns within the genre of mathematical language. As noted above, investigation of the language of mathematics can also develop in students a curiosity about language and deepen their understanding of how words work. Three strategies for extending students' knowledge of the language of mathematics are outlined below.

A. Creating mathematical language banks
Students can systematically collect the meanings of words and phrases they encounter in mathematical texts in a personal or group *language bank.* Ideally, the language bank would be created in a series of files within the classroom computer but it can also be done with paper and pencil in a class notebook.

Paradoxically, the complexity of mathematical language provides some important opportunities for language exploration. As mentioned above, a large percentage of the less frequent academic and technical vocabulary of English derives from Latin and Greek roots. One implication of this is that word formation follows some very predictable patterns. These patterns are similar in English and Spanish.

When students know some of the rules or conventions of how academic words are formed, it gives them an edge in extending their vocabulary. It helps them figure out not only the meanings of individual words but also how to form different parts of speech from those words.

A central aspect of academic language is *nominalization*. This refers to the process whereby abstract nouns are formed from verbs and adjectives. Take, for example, four common verbs that occur in the math curriculum: *multiply, divide, measure,* and *equal.* The word families (excluding verb forms and plurals) for each of these words are presented below.

Verb	Noun	Adjective
multiply	multiplication multiple multiplicity	multiple
divide	division dividend	divisive divided
measure	measure measurement	measured
equal equalize	equality equal equalizer	equal equitable

We see in these four word families, several common ways in which the English language forms nouns from verbs. One pattern is to add the suffix *-tion* or *-ion* to the verb form as in *multiplication, division,* and many other mathematical terms, such as *estimation, notation,* and *operation.* Another pattern is to add the suffix *-ment* as in *measurement,* while a third pattern is to add the suffix *-ity* or *-ty* as in *equality, capacity, property,* and *probability.* When we demystify how this academic language works, students are more likely to recognize parts of speech in their reading of complex texts across the curriculum and to become more adept at inferring meaning from context. For example, when a student recognizes that *acceleration* is a noun (rather than a verb or an adjective), he or she is one step closer to understanding the meaning of the term in the context of a particular sentence or text.

Students can be encouraged to use dictionaries (in both English and their L1, when available) to explore the more subtle meanings of these mathematical words. For example, students could be asked to work in pairs or small groups to think through the differences in meaning between the verbs *equal* and *equalize;* among the nouns *equality, equal,* and *equalizer;* and between the adjectives *equal* and *equitable.*

This nominalization process also permits us to think in terms of abstract realities or states and to use higher-level cognitive functions that require uses of language very different from the conversational or "playground" language that we acquire in everyday situations. This point is made clearly by Pauline Gibbons:

> The playground situation does not normally offer children the opportunity to use such language as: *if we increase the angle by 5 degrees, we could cut the circumference into equal parts.* Nor does it normally require the language associated with the higher-order thinking skills, such as hypothesizing, evaluating, inferring, generalizing, predicting, or classifying. Yet these are the language functions which are related to learning and the development of cognition; they occur in all areas of the curriculum, and without them a child's potential in academic areas cannot be realized (1991, p. 3).

Gibbons goes on to point out that explicit modeling of academic language is particularly important in schools with large numbers of ESL students:

> In such a school it is very easy to fall into the habit of constantly simplifying our language because we expect not to be understood. But if we only ever use basic language such as *put in* or *take out* or *go faster,* some children will not have any opportunity to learn other ways of expressing these ideas, such as *insert* or *remove* or *accelerate.* And these are the words that are needed to refer to the general concepts related to the ideas, such as *removal, insertion,* and *acceleration* (1991, p. 18).

In short, when students know some of the rules or conventions of how academic words are formed, it gives them an edge in extending their vocabulary. It helps them figure out not only the meanings of individual words but also how to form different parts of speech from these words. One way of organizing students' language detective work in mathematics is to focus separately on *meaning, form,* and *use.* Working in pairs or small groups, students can be encouraged to collect and explore one mathematics word per day, focusing on one or more of these three categories.

- **Focus on Meaning** Categories that can be explored within a Focus on Meaning include *Mathematical meaning; Everyday meaning; Meaning in other subject areas; L1 equivalents; Related words in L1 (cognates); Synonyms; Antonyms; Homonyms; Meaning of prefix; Meaning of root;* and *Meaning of suffix.* Not all of these categories will be relevant for every word, but considered together they provide a map of directions that an exploration of meaning might pursue. Take a possible exploration of the word *subtract:*

Mathematical meaning:	take one number or quantity from another (or compare two numbers or quantities)
L1 equivalent (Spanish):	restar, sustraer
Synonym:	deduct
Antonym:	add
Meaning of prefix:	under or away
Meaning of root:	from the Latin for "pull"

- **Focus on Form** Most of the root words in mathematics that come from Latin and Greek form not just one part of speech; we can make nouns, verbs, and adjectives from many of these root words. If we know the typical patterns for forming nouns and adjectives from root verbs, we can recognize these parts of speech when they appear in text. The implications for expanding students' vocabulary are clear: rather than learning just one word in isolation, students are enabled to learn entire *word families,* a process that can dramatically expand their working vocabulary.

  Categories that can be explored within a Focus on Form include *Word family and grammatical patterns; Words with the same prefix; Words with the same root;* and *Words with the same suffix.* Consider again the word *subtract:*

Word family/ grammatical patterns:	subtract, subtracts, subtracted, subtracting (verb forms)
	subtraction, subtractions (noun forms)
Words with same prefix:	substitute, subtotal, suburban, subway
Words with same root:	tractor, traction

- **Focus on Use** Students can explore the range of uses of particular words through brainstorming as a class or small group; looking words up in dictionaries, encyclopedias, or thesauri; or asking parents or other adults outside of school. Categories that can be explored within a Focus on Use include *General uses; Idioms; Metaphorical uses; Proverbs; Advertisements; Puns;* and *Jokes.* For the word *subtract,* most students will not find much that will fall within these categories other than the category of *general uses.* However, with some of the more frequent words in mathematical discourse that derive from the Anglo-Saxon lexicon of English rather than the Greek/Latin lexicon, many of these other categories will yield a multitude of examples. Consider the multiple meanings and figurative uses of words such as *great* (as in "greater than"), *big,* and *double* that students might explore.

  In short, when students explore the language of mathematics by collecting specimens of mathematical language in a systematic and cumulative way, they expand not only their understanding of mathematical terms and concepts but also their knowledge of how the English language works (e.g., the fact that abstract nouns are often formed in English by adding the suffix *-tion* to the verb). The development of language awareness in this way will benefit students' reading comprehension and writing ability across the curriculum.

B. Taking ownership of mathematical language by means of "reporting back"

If students are to take ownership of mathematical language, we must provide ample opportunities and encouragement for them to use this language for authentic purposes in the classroom. In the absence of active use of the language, students' grasp of the mathematical register is likely to remain shallow and passive.

Researchers (e.g., Swain, 1997) have noted three ways in which L2 acquisition is stimulated by active use of the language:

- Students must try to figure out sophisticated aspects of the target language in order to express what they want to communicate.

- It highlights to both students and teachers the aspects of language the students still find troublesome.

- It provides teachers with the opportunity to provide corrective feedback to build language awareness and help students figure out how the language works.

- **Have Students Report Back Orally and in Writing** One example of how this process operates in the teaching of content areas such as mathematics is provided by Gibbons (1991). She emphasizes the importance of *reporting back* as a strategy for promoting academic language development. For example, after a concrete, hands-on group experience or project, students are asked to report back to the class orally about what they did and observed and then to write about it. As students progress from concrete, hands-on experience to more abstract oral and written language use, they must include sufficient information within the language itself for the meaning to be understood by those who did not share in the original experience. She notes that

> while hands-on experiences are a very valuable starting point for language development, they do not, on their own, offer children adequate opportunities to develop the more 'context-free' language associated with reading and writing.... [A] reporting-back situation is a bridge into the more formal demands of literacy. It allows children to try out in speech—in a realistic and authentic situation—the sort of language they meet in books and which they need to develop in their writing. Where children's own language background has not led to this extension of oral language, it becomes even more important for the classroom to provide such opportunities (1991, p. 31).

In short, students become more aware of the cognitive processes and strategies they use to solve math problems, and they are enabled to take ownership of the language that reflects and facilitates these cognitive processes, when the curriculum provides extensive opportunities for them to explain orally and in written form what they did and how they did it.

C. Mastering the language of mathematical assessment

- **Have Students Create Test Items** High-stakes testing has become a fact of life in classrooms across the United States, and consequently a large majority of curriculum materials include not only formative assessment integrated within the curriculum unit but also practice oriented to performance on state-wide standardized tests. Consistent with the emphasis on providing opportunities for students to take ownership of the language of mathematics through active use of that language, we can also encourage students to gain insight and control over the language of mathematical assessment. We can do this by having students create their own multiple-choice (or other relevant) tests in mathematics rather than always being on the receiving end of tests that adults have created. The process might work as follows.

In order to familiarize students with the process (and also have some fun in a friendly, competitive context), we can have them work in heterogeneous groups to construct their own tests, initially on topics with which they are familiar or on which they have carried out research. For example, the teacher might explain how multiple-choice items are constructed (e.g., the role of distractors), and each group might construct a set of approximately 5 items on topics such as baseball, popular music, television programs, or popular slang. These items are then pooled and the entire set of items is administered as a test to the entire class. Subsequently, each group might research aspects of a particular content area and construct items based on their research. In the context of math, groups could construct test items that focus on the unit of study (e.g., fractions or decimals) that has just been completed. An incentive system could be instituted such that the groups gain points based on their performance on the pooled test that leads ultimately to some reward.

The rationale for this reversal of roles is that construction of test items is more cognitively challenging (and engaging) than simply responding to test items. In order to come up with items that will be challenging for the other groups, students must know the content of the unit in an active rather than a passive way. The within-group discussion and collaboration in generating the items and distractors is also likely to reinforce both language and content knowledge for all students in the group, but particularly for those students (likely including some ESL students) whose grasp of the content may be fragile.

Within this conception, standardized math tests are viewed as one particular genre of math language. Students should be familiar with the conventions of this genre if their academic worth is to be recognized. In generating multiple-choice test items, students are developing language awareness in the context of a highly challenging (but engaging) cognitive activity.

The same principle can be applied to the creation of other forms of assessment that tap both math and language concepts. For example, teachers could have students create multiple-choice cloze sentences that reflect both everyday and math-specific meanings of mathematical vocabulary.

1. Five _____ six _____ eleven.
2. On the _____ side, my share _____ his.
3. On the _____ side, his share is _____ mine.
4. Numbers less than zero are called _____ numbers.
5. When we multiply by two, we _____ the quantity.

Target Words
plus
double
equals
negative

Conclusion

Mathematics will assume relevance to students and be learned much more effectively when they can relate the content to their prior experience and current interests. In addition to activating students' prior knowledge and building background, we may need to modify our instruction in specific ways to make the content accessible to ESL students who are still in the process of catching up to native speakers in academic English- language proficiency. This catch-up process will typically take at least 5 years, partly because students are catching up to a moving target—native speakers of English are not standing still, waiting for ESL students to bridge the gap. Thus, even ESL students who are relatively fluent in English may require specific support in accessing mathematical concepts and problems expressed in English.

These supports should focus not only on making the mathematics content comprehensible to students but also on extending their awareness of how the language of mathematics works. In this way, students can develop insights about academic language that will bear fruit in other content areas (e.g., reading comprehension in language arts and vocabulary building in social studies). A goal of this process of extending students' command of academic language is to enable them to take ownership of the language of the curriculum and use it for authentic purposes. Thus, they will benefit from opportunities to carry out projects and explain what they did both orally and in written form. As the audience becomes more distant (e.g., in the case of a more formal written report), students are required to use more abstract, explicit, and precise language to communicate their meaning. When we integrate these active uses of language with the mathematics curriculum, students benefit both with respect to mathematics and to language facility.

References

Collier, V. P. and Thomas, W. P. (1999). Making U.S. schools effective for English language learners, Part 1. *TESOL Matters,* 9:4 (August/September), pp. 1 & 6.

Cummins (2001). *Negotiating identities: Education for empowerment in a diverse society.* 2nd edition. Los Angeles: California Association for Bilingual Education.

Díaz-Rico, L. & Weed, K. Z. (2002). *The crosscultural, language, and academic development handbook: A complete K–12 reference guide.* 2nd edition. Boston: Allyn & Bacon.

Gibbons, P. (1991). *Learning to learn in a second language.* Newtown, Australia: Primary English Teaching Association.

Meyer, L. (2000). Barriers to meaningful instruction for English learners. *Theory into Practice,* 34(2), 228–236.

Swain, M. (1997). Collaborative dialogue: Its contribution to second language learning. *Revista Canaria de Estudios Ingleses,* 34, 115–132.

© Pearson Education, Inc., 5

Place Value Through Billions

USE WITH LESSON
1-1

ACCESS CONTENT; EXTEND LANGUAGE

Objective Write the standard, word, and expanded forms of whole numbers to billions, and identify the value of digits in whole numbers.

Materials 5 index cards labeled with place values from ones to ten thousands; tape

Vocabulary Place value, digit, value

ESL Strategies | **Use before** CHECK ✓ | ⏱ 10 MIN

Use Graphic Organizers ➤ Distribute one place-value index card to each of five student volunteers. Write 41,962 on the board. Read the number aloud. **I will point to a digit in this number. If your card tells the digit's place value, tape your card above the digit.** Each time a student tapes a card to the board, ask: **What is the value of this digit?** To help them answer, ask: **If the digit 4 is in the ten thousands place, what is its value?** *(40 thousand)*

Continue until all 5 place-value names are taped above the number. Tell students that they have made a place-value chart.

Have Students Report Back Orally ➤ Write 96,812 on the board under the place-value cards. Point to a digit in the number, beginning with the ones column and ending with the ten thousands column. With each digit, ask a student to read the place value and give the digit's value.

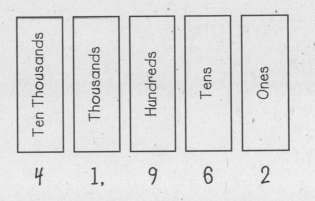

Comparing and Ordering Whole Numbers

USE WITH LESSON
1-2

ACCESS CONTENT

Objective Compare and order whole numbers through millions.

Materials Place-value models: ones, tens, and hundreds.

Use before [LEARN]

🕐 15 MIN

Use ➤ Write the number 243 on the board. Model the number using :ones, tens,
Demonstration and hundreds. **There is a 2 in the hundreds place. I need 2 hundreds.**
How many tens will I need? Explain your answer. *(4, because there is a*
4 in the tens place) **How many ones? Explain your answer.** *(3, because*
there is a 3 in the ones place)

Let's compare 243 with 215. Which number has more hundreds ?
(They both have 2.) **Which number has more tens ?** *(243 has more*
tens rods.) **Which number is greater?** *(243)*

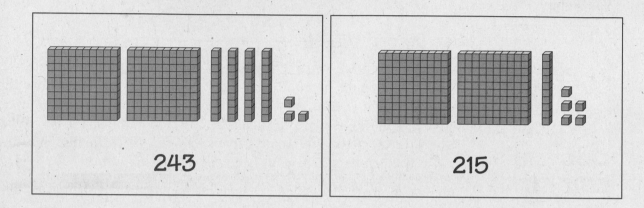

243   215

Use Manipulatives ➤ Have students model and compare 351 and 309. Remind them to compare
the hundreds first, then tens, and then ones in each number and decide
which number is greater. Ask students to explain their thinking as they solve
the problem.

Place Value Through
Thousandths

USE WITH LESSON
1-3

EXTEND LANGUAGE; ACCESS CONTENT

Objective Write decimals in standard, word, and expanded form through
thousandths, identify the value of digits in decimal numbers, and name
equivalent decimals.

Materials *(per pair)* Index cards with the terms *tenths, hundredths,* and
thousandths

Vocabulary Tenths, hundredths, thousandths

ESL Strategies **Use before** [LEARN]

🕐 5 MIN

Focus on Form ➤ Pronounce the words <u>tenths</u>, <u>hundredths</u>, and <u>thousandths</u>. Have students
repeat after you. Explain that these are place values to the right of the
decimal point.

Use Graphic ➤ Write the number 0.842 on the board. Point to the 8. **This is eight tenths.**
Organizers Divide the class into pairs. Distribute a set of place-value index cards to

each pair. Have a student from each pair hold up the correct place-value card. Check each pair's response.

Repeat for the other two digits. This time, have students tell you the place values for the digits. Add a zero to the right of 0.842 (0.8420). **Does this change the value of the number?** *(No)* Have students explain why.

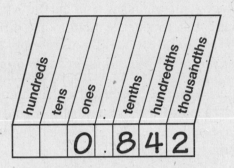

Comparing and Ordering Decimals

USE WITH LESSON 1-4

ACTIVATE PRIOR KNOWLEDGE/BUILD BACKGROUND; ACCESS CONTENT

Objective Compare and order decimals through thousandths.

ESL Strategies   *Use before* **LEARN**   🕐 10–15 MIN

Connect to Prior Knowledge of Math ➤ Write 852 and 857 on the board. Invite a volunteer to use his or her prior knowledge to compare 852 with 857. Remind students that they know how to compare numbers using place value.

Write 852.453 and 852.617 on the board. **You can compare in the same way for digits after the decimal point. How can you compare 852.453 with 852.617?** *(Compare the digits in the tenths place)* **Which number is greater?** *(852.617)* **How do you know?** *(Six tenths is greater than four tenths.)*

Use Small-Group Interactions ➤ Divide the class into pairs. Have one student write 2 six-digit decimal numbers on the paper and the second student say which is greater. Then have the students change tasks. Encourage them to discuss their answers.

Place-Value Patterns

USE WITH LESSON 1-5

EXTEND LANGUAGE

Objective Use place-value ideas to write multiples of 100, 1,000, and 10,000 in different ways.

Use before CHECK ✓

🕐 20 MIN

Have Students Report Back Orally ➤ Write 10, 100, 1,000, and 10,000 on the board vertically. **What do you notice as I write the next number?** *(You add another zero.)* Explain that to get the next number you multiply by 10.

Have Students Create Test Items ➤ Have students work in small groups to create three test items related to place-value patterns. Students may write exercises like the ones on the page, but encourage them to use different numbers than they used in the examples.

Explain that you will choose five of the submitted exercises to make a short quiz. **You get one point for each correct answer on the quiz. You get one extra point if I use a question your group wrote.** When all the groups have submitted their exercises, choose a broad selection and administer the quiz.

Problem-Solving Skill: Read and Understand

USE WITH LESSON

1-6

ACTIVATE PRIOR KNOWLEDGE/BUILD BACKGROUND; ACCESS CONTENT

Objective Tell in words what is known and what needs to be determined in given word problems.

ESL Strategies

Use before LEARN

🕐 10 MIN

Use Literature ➤ Have students read the paragraph on Student Book Page 18. **What is the question in the reading?** *(What year is the Blue Angels' 50th anniversary?)*

Paraphrase Ideas ➤ Ask questions that will help students answer the question from the reading. **What year did the Blue Angels begin flying?** *(1946)* **How many years did they fly before the anniversary?** *(50)* Organize their answers on the board. **What year was the Blue Angels' 50th anniversary?** *(1996)* **Tell how you answered the question.**

start year	+	years flying	=	50th anniversary
1946	+	50	=	?

Adding and Subtracting Mentally

ACTIVATE PRIOR KNOWLEDGE/BUILD BACKGROUND; ACCESS CONTENT

Objective Compute sums and differences mentally using the Commutative and Associative Properties of Addition, compatible numbers, and compensation, and by counting up.

Vocabulary Compensation

⌐ ESL Strategies ⌐   ***Use before*** LEARN   ⏱ 10 MIN

Connect to Prior Knowledge of Language ➤ Relate <u>compensation</u> to borrowing. **If I borrow a dollar from you this week, I must compensate by giving a dollar back next week.** Have students use the word *compensate* in a sentence about borrowing. Then ask students to share their ideas of what the word *compensate* means. (*Make up for*)

Use Demonstration ➤ Write the expression $299 + 57$ on the board. **It is easier to add mentally with 300 than with 299. I can add 1.** Write $299 + 1 = 300$. **But I must make up for it, or compensate, by subtracting 1 from 57.** Write $57 - 1 = 56$. Write $(299 + 1) + (57 - 1) = 300 + 56$. **Now it is easy to add these numbers in my head. Ask a volunteer for the solution.** (*356*)

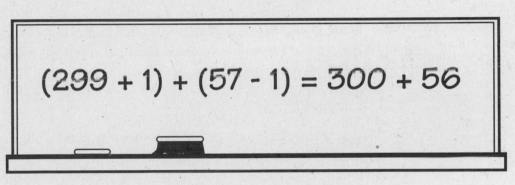

$$(299 + 1) + (57 - 1) = 300 + 56$$

Write the expression $501 + 78$ on the board. Have a volunteer explain how to mentally add by compensating, and solve the problem. (*579*)

Rounding Whole Numbers and Decimals

ACCESS CONTENT

Objective Round whole numbers through millions and decimals through thousandths.

Materials (*per group*) 5 index cards with decimal numbers in thousandths

Vocabulary Rounding

Use before CHECK ✓

🕐 15 MIN

Use ➤
Demonstration

Write the number 4.862 in large print on the board. We want to <u>round</u> **to the nearest tenth.** Have a volunteer come to the board and underline the digit in the tenths place. *(8)* **To do this we look at the digit to the right of the 8.** Have a second volunteer circle this digit. *(6)* **Is this digit greater than or less than 5?** *(Greater than 5)* **So, we round the tenths digit up.** Have a third volunteer write the rounded number on the board. *(4.9)*

Use Small-Group ➤
Interactions

Divide the class into 4 or 5 groups. Write the number 7.135 on the board. Below each digit, from left to right, write the words "whole number", "tenths", "hundredths", and "thousandths" on the board. Distribute 5 decimal number index cards to each group. Have a member of the group select a card from the stack. **Round the decimal number on the card to the nearest whole number.** Point to the digit 7 on the board. Ask the group to work together to check each answer and make corrections if necessary.

Have a different student turn over the next number card, and repeat the activity as you point to each place value on the board. Continue the activity until each group has rounded the numbers on the 5 cards.

Estimating Sums and Differences

USE WITH LESSON
1-9

ACTIVATE PRIOR KNOWLEDGE/BUILD BACKGROUND; ACCESS CONTENT

Objective Use rounding, front-end estimation, and front-end estimation with adjusting to estimate sums and differences of whole numbers and decimals.

Vocabulary Front-end estimation

Use before LEARN

🕐 10 MIN

Connect to Prior ➤
Knowledge of
Math

An estimate is a guess. Explain that estimates can make numbers easier to work with. Write 87,625 + 2,321 on the board. Have students say the equation aloud with you. **This is not easy to add in my head. I can round**

the numbers to **87,000 and 2,000.** Write 87,000 + 2000 = 89,000. **Since the numbers were rounded, this is not an exact answer. We call this an estimate.**

Use Gestures ➤ Tell students that they will learn to use <u>front-end estimation</u> to estimate sums and differences. Write 683 on the board. Have students say the number aloud with you. **Point to the front of this number. Why is this the front of the number?** *(You read numbers from left to right.)* **What is the front-end digit?** *(6)* Explain that in front-end estimation, all digits are changed to zero except for the front-end digit. **What is the front-end estimate for 683?** *(600)*

front ➞ 683

Problem Solving Skill: Plan and Solve

USE WITH LESSON 1-10

EXTEND LANGUAGE; ACTIVATE PRIOR KNOWLEDGE/BUILD BACKGROUND

Objective Give appropriate strategies and alternate strategies for solving word problems.

ESL Strategies   *Use before* CHECK ✓   ⏱ 10 MIN

Have Students ➤ Ask students to list the steps that they take to get ready for school each
Report Back morning. Suggest entries for them: make bed, get dressed, eat breakfast
in Writing Encourage them to be as detailed as possible. **Making a list like this can help you solve a problem.** Have students write down how much time it takes to perform each activity. Then have two student volunteers write their lists on the board.

Use ➤ **How can a list help me solve a problem?** *(It can help to organize the*
Brainstorming *important information.)* Write the questions shown on the board.

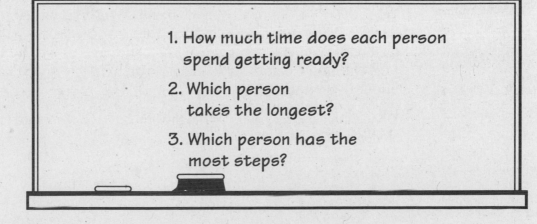

1. How much time does each person spend getting ready?

2. Which person takes the longest?

3. Which person has the most steps?

Have students answer the questions using the two lists on the board. Then have students write and solve other problems that can be answered using the lists.

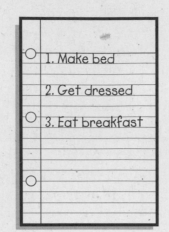

Adding and Subtracting Whole Numbers

ACCESS CONTENT

USE WITH LESSON 1-11

Objective Compute sums and differences of two whole numbers greater than 10,000.

Materials *(per pair)* Two empty egg cartons (with 2 cups cut off of each); 15 counters

ESL Strategies | *Use before* **LEARN** | ⏱ 15 MIN

Use Real Objects ➤ Divide the class into pairs. **We need to fill the cartons with all 15 counters.** Have them take turns placing a counter in each slot of the carton. **What do we do when the carton is full?** *(Start filling the next one)* Explain that there is now 1 whole carton, with 10 counters, and 1 carton that is partially filled, with 5 counters. **This is an example of regrouping.**

Use ➤ Demonstration

Write 999 + 43 vertically on the board. **What is 9 added to 3?** *(12)* Explain that you can regroup 12 as 1 ten and 2 ones as you write this on the board. **You can bring down the 2 ones and move the 1 ten into the tens column.** Continue with the problem in this way. Explain how each digit is regrouped.

Divide the class into pairs. Write the problems on the board and have students solve them.

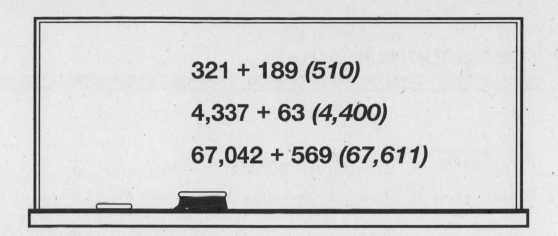

$$321 + 189 \; (510)$$

$$4,337 + 63 \; (4,400)$$

$$67,042 + 569 \; (67,611)$$

For each problem, have one partner explain to the other how he or she solved by regrouping.

Adding Decimals

USE WITH LESSON 1-12

ACCESS CONTENT

Objective Compute sums of decimals involving tenths, hundredths, and thousandths.

Materials *(per student)* Decimal Place-Value Charts (Teaching Tool 2); scissors; tape

ESL Strategies

Use before **CHECK** ✓   ⏱ 10 MIN

Use Graphic Organizers ➤ Have students cut, combine, and tape three decimal place-value charts into a vertical column. Write $1.43 + 2.16$ on the board. **Can this problem fit in the chart? How?** *(Write 1.43 in the top row and 2.16 below it.)* **Write the numbers in the chart.** Have students add the digits in the hundredths column. **What is the sum? Where do you write the answer?** *(3 + 6 = 9; In the hundredths box of the bottom row)* Repeat for the tenths and ones columns, working from right to left.

Use Small-Group Interactions ➤ Divide the class into small groups. Write $1.75 + 1.12$ on the board. Have students work together to repeat the activity for this addition problem.

	1	.	7	5
+	1	.	1	2
	2	.	8	7

Subtracting Decimals

ACTIVATE PRIOR KNOWLEDGE/BUILD BACKGROUND

Objective Compute differences of decimals involving tenths, hundredths, and thousandths.

ESL Strategies | **Use before** LEARN | ⏱ 5 MIN

Connect to Prior Knowledge of Math ➤ Have students compare the decimals 1.2 and 1.20. Students can use decimal model sheets or other manipulatives. Be sure they understand that the decimal numbers are equivalent. **Does the 0 after the 2 in 1.20 change the value of the number? Explain.** (*No; Putting extra zeros after the last number in the decimal is just another way of writing the number.*)

Use Brainstorming ➤ Write $2.5 - 1.34$ vertically on the board, aligning the decimal points. **In 2.5 there is no digit in the hundredths column.** Ask students to come up with ideas about how to rewrite the problem so that they can subtract. Make sure students understand that 2.5 can be rewritten as 2.50 since both numbers have the same value. Write $2.50 - 1.34$ vertically on the board. **Now the place values line up.** Have a volunteer come to the board to solve the problem. (*1.16*)

$$\begin{array}{r} 2.50 \\ -1.34 \\ \hline \end{array}$$

Problem-Solving Skill: Look Back and Check

ACCESS CONTENT; EXTEND LANGUAGE

Objective Tell whether and why the work shown for given problems is correct or not.

ESL Strategies | **Use before** LEARN | ⏱ 5 MIN

Use Pantomime ➤ **After you finish a problem, it is a good idea to look back at what you did and check the answer.** Have students pantomime *look back* and discuss what it means. **What will you do when you look back at a problem?**

(Sample answer: Go back to the beginning and make sure I answered the original question)

Focus on Use ➤ Have students discuss what it means to check something. **What does it mean to check an answer?** *(Make sure the answer is correct.)* **How could you check an answer?** *(Possible answers: I will make sure I did each step correctly; I will solve the problem another way and see if I get the same answer.)*

Problem-Solving Applications: Cruise Ships

ACCESS CONTENT

Objective Review and apply key concepts, skills, and strategies learned in this and previous chapters.

ESL Strategies | ***Use before*** **LEARN**   🕐 10 MIN

Use Small-Group Interactions ➤ Write the following word problem on the board, excluding the answer, and then read it aloud.

> **"Some of the world's largest passenger ships were the 882-foot S.S. Titanic, the 1,029-foot S.S. Normandic, the 726-foot S.S. Baltic, the 1,031-foot Queen Elizabeth, and the 790-foot S.S. Lusitania. List the ships in order from least to greatest in length. How much longer was the largest ship than the smallest ship?"**
> *(Baltic, Lusitania, Titanic, Normandie, Queen Elizabeth; 305 feet)*

Have students work in small groups to plan their strategies for solving the problem. Have them write down the steps they use, for example, "First compare and order the lengths. Then subtract the least length from the greatest length." Ask each group to share its work with a neighboring group. Have students compare their written plans and solutions.

Multiplication Patterns

ACTIVATE PRIOR KNOWLEDGE/BUILD BACKGROUND

Objective Mentally compute products of whole numbers using patterns and multiplication properties.

Materials Colored chalk

Vocabulary Commutative Property, Associative Property

ESL Strategies   *Use before* **LEARN**   ⏱ 10 MIN

Connect to Prior ➤ Remind students that they learned about the <u>Commutative Property</u> of
Knowledge of   Addition. **What does this property tell you?** *(You can change the order of*
Math   *the numbers being added without changing the answer.)* **What do you think**
                the Commutative Property of Multiplication tells you? *(You can change*
                the order of the numbers being multiplied without changing the answer.)

Connect to Prior ➤ Write $(2 \times 3) \times 5 = 2 \times (3 \times 5)$ on the board. **Associates are numbers**
Knowledge of   **that are grouped together. The parentheses show which numbers are**
Language   **associates. Which two numbers are associates on the left side?** *(2 and 3)*
                On the right side? *(3 and 5)* **What do you think <u>Associative Property</u>** of
                Multiplication means? *(You can group the numbers being multiplied in*
                different ways without changing the answer.)

Associative Property of Multiplication

$(2 \times 3) \times 5 = 2 \times (3 \times 5)$

Estimating Products

USE WITH LESSON 2-2

ACCESS CONTENT

Objective Use rounding and compatible numbers to estimate products of whole numbers, and identify estimates as overestimates or underestimates.

Materials Paper clips

Vocabulary Overestimate, underestimate

Use before **LEARN**   ⏲ 10 MIN

Use Real Objects ➤ **What is an estimate?** *(A guess for an answer or a number)* **What is an overestimate?** *(A guess that is higher than the answer)* **What is an underestimate?** *(A guess that is lower than the answer)*

Divide the class into groups and give each group a large pile of paper clips. **Estimate the number of clips in this pile.** Have each student write an estimate of the number of paper clips, then have group members count the actual number and discuss which estimates were closest. **Did you overestimate or underestimate? Explain.** *(Students should explain that overestimates are higher than the actual number and underestimates are lower than the actual number.)* Repeat the activity with a different number of paper clips.

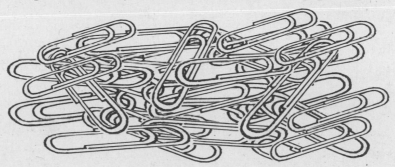

Mental Math: Using the Distributive Property

ACCESS CONTENT

USE WITH LESSON **2-3**

Objective Mentally multiply numbers of up to three places by numbers of up to two places.

Vocabulary Distributive Property

ESL Strategies   *Use before* **LEARN**   ⏲ 10 MIN

Use Real Objects ➤ Hold up a stack of 8 papers. Bring 4 volunteers to the front of the class. **I am going to distribute 2 papers to each student.** Distribute the papers, giving 1 paper at a time to each student. Have volunteers take turns following instructions for distributing papers. For example, have a volunteer distribute 9 papers among 3 students. Give each student an opportunity to role-play the activity. **What does** *distribute* **mean?** *(Spread out, hand out, deliver, divide among)*

Use Graphic ➤ Write "Distributive Property" and $3 \times (4 + 2)$ on the board.
Organizers

You can use the Distributive Property to distribute numbers in problems like this one. Let's distribute the 3 to the 4 and the 2. Draw an arrow from the 3 to the 4 and write 3×4 on the left side below the original problem. Draw an arrow from the 3 to the 2 and write 3×2 on the right side below the problem. Write a + sign between the two expressions. **Explain how we**

distributed the 3 to the 4 and the 2. *(We multiplied the 3 times both numbers and added the products.)* Repeat the process with $2 \times (3 + 5)$, then have volunteers complete and explain the steps for additional examples.

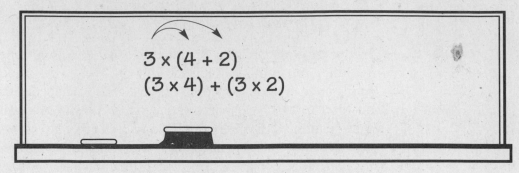

$$3 \times (4 + 2)$$
$$(3 \times 4) + (3 \times 2)$$

Multiplying Whole Numbers

USE WITH LESSON 2-4

ACTIVATE PRIOR KNOWLEDGE/BUILD BACKGROUND; ACCESS CONTENT

Objective Use the standard algorithm to multiply numbers by one- and two-digit numbers.

Materials *(per student)* 2 different colored index cards

ESL Strategies

Use before **LEARN**

⏱ 5 MIN

Connect to Prior Knowledge of Language ➤ Write $23 \times 9 = 207$ on the board. Remind students that a number being multiplied is called a *factor* and the answer is the *product*. Invite students to repeat the words "factor" and "product" after you. Point to 23 and hold up a card showing the word "factor." Repeat for the number 9. Then point to 207 and hold up a card showing "product."

Give Frequent Feedback ➤ Have students write "factor" on a colored index card and "product" on the different color card. Point to the 9 in $23 \times 9 = 207$. **Is this number a factor or a product? Hold up the card that shows the correct answer.** *(Factor)* Repeat for 207. Check that students show the "product" card. Repeat with other numbers in a variety of multiplication sentences. Tell the class the correct answer each time, after you scan the responses on the cards.

$$23 \quad \times \quad 9 \quad = \quad 207$$
factor   factor   product

Choose a Computation Method

USE WITH LESSON 2-5

ACCESS CONTENT

Objective For a variety of problems, state the computation method to be used and add or subtract using that method.

Materials *(per student)* Calculator

ESL Strategies ⎞ *Use before* **LEARN** ⏱ 10 MIN

Use Real Objects ➤ A <u>calculator</u> **is a machine that can add, subtract, multiply, divide, and perform other kinds of math operations.** Give each student a calculator. Show them how to turn it on/off and clear the display.

Use Small-Group Interactions ➤

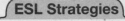

Press the 7 key. Have students show each other their displays and check that the proper key was pressed. Encourage students to help each other make corrections if necessary. Repeat with a variety of commands, gradually increasing in complexity. Give volunteers the opportunity to announce the commands. Be sure that students clear the display before each new command. For example: **Show the number 485. Press the key you use to subtract. Show the number 117. Press the key that shows the equal sign. What answer do you see?** *(368)* **Press the key to clear. Turn the calculator off.**

Problem-Solving Strategy:
Make an Organized List

USE WITH LESSON 2-6

ACTIVATE PRIOR KNOWLEDGE/BUILD BACKGROUND; ACCESS CONTENT

Objective Use organized lists to solve word problems, and write answers in complete sentences.

Materials 3 chairs

ESL Strategies ⎞ *Use before* **LEARN** ⏱ 15 MIN

Connect to Prior Experiences ➤ **Name a type of list you might use in real life.** *(Sample answers: grocery list, list of friends' phone numbers)* **What does a list do?** *(A list organizes information.)* Tell students that one way to solve difficult problems is to make a list of the possible answers.

Use Total Physical Response ➤ Place 3 chairs at the front of the room. Ask 1 volunteer to keep a list on the board and 3 others to participate in the demonstration. **We want to organize these people for a photograph. They must sit in the chairs and the chairs cannot be moved. How many different ways can they be arranged? What are the ways?** *(6; ABC, ACB, BAC, BCA, CAB, CBA)*

Let the students discuss the different arrangements, and have the volunteers take their places as instructed. Be sure that the recorder writes down each new arrangement, either using names or letters. Guide students to recognize when a pattern has been repeated by checking the list. End the activity when students recognize that they have found all 6 arrangements. **How did the list help us solve the problem?** *(It organized the information and gave us a way to check new combinations.)*

Decimal Patterns

USE WITH LESSON 2-7

ACCESS CONTENT

Objective Mentally multiply any decimal by a power of ten.

Materials *(per group)* Index cards numbered 0–9; index card with a decimal point

ESL Strategies

Use before **LEARN**

🕐 5 MIN

Paraphrase Ideas ➤ Remind students that a pattern is something that repeats according to a rule. Write these multiplication facts on the board.

$$3.714 \times 1 = 3.714$$
$$3.714 \times 10 = 37.14$$
$$3.714 \times 100 = 371.4$$
$$3.714 \times 1,000 = 3,714$$

Use Manipulatives ➤ Emphasize that there is a pattern to the answers when multiplying a decimal by 10, 100, and 1,000. **Look at how the decimal point moves when you multiply by 10, 100, and 1,000. What pattern do you see?** *(You move the decimal point one place to the right for each zero in 10, 100, or 1,000.)*

Divide the class into small groups. Write 5.682 on the board, and have each group use the cards to model the number on a desk or table. **Move the decimal point to show the answer when you multiply this number by 10.** *(Check that students show 56.82 with the cards.)* **How many places to the right did you move the decimal point?** *(One place)* Have students return the decimal point card to the original location and repeat the activity for multiplying by 100 and 1,000. Repeat with 4.905 and 6.237.

| 5 | . | 6 | 8 | 2 |

Estimating Decimal Products

USE WITH LESSON 2-8

ACTIVATE PRIOR KNOWLEDGE/BUILD BACKGROUND; ACCESS CONTENT

Objective Use rounding and compatible numbers to estimate products of decimal numbers, and identify estimates as overestimates or underestimates.

Materials *(per group)* 6 index cards with decimal numbers on them; blank cube labeled "round up" on 3 sides and "round down" on 3 sides

Use before **LEARN**　　　　　　　　　　🕐 10 MIN

Connect to Prior ➤ Remind students that they know how to round whole numbers and decimals.
Knowledge of Math Explain that rounding is one way to estimate an answer in a decimal
multiplication problem. **Why would you estimate the product?** *(Sample
answers: I might not need an exact answer; I could use the estimate to see if
my answer is reasonable, or makes sense.)*

Write 1.54 on the board. Review the difference between rounding up and
rounding down. **What is this number rounded up?** *(1.6 or 2)* **What is this
number rounded down?** *(1.5 or 1)*

Use Small Group ➤ Assign students to groups. Have each group choose one of the index cards.
Interactions Direct each student to roll the number cube and follow the directions to either
round the number on the index card up or down. Have students write their
answers, then share them with the group. The group should work together to
evaluate and correct any errors. Repeat the activity for each of the cards.

Multiplying Whole Numbers and Decimals

USE WITH LESSON 2-9

ACCESS CONTENT

Objective Use partial products and the standard algorithm to multiply whole
numbers by decimals.

Materials *(per pair)* 2 index cards

Use before **LEARN**　　　　　　　　　　🕐 5 MIN

Use ➤ Explain that the number of decimal places in a number is the number of digits
Demonstration to the right of the decimal point, including zeros. Write 16.73 on the board.
Point to the decimal point and say: **This is the decimal point.** Point to the 7,
then the 3 and count aloud: **1, 2. There are 2 digits to the right of the decimal
point. How many decimal places does this number have?** *(2 places)* Repeat
the demonstration for the numbers 4.152 *(3 places)*, 197.5 *(1 place)*, 0.804
(3 places), and 1.30 *(2 places)*. Have students count the places aloud.

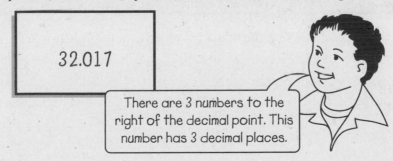

32.017

There are 3 numbers to the right of the decimal point. This number has 3 decimal places.

Divide the class into pairs. Have one partner write a decimal number on an index card. Then have the other partner say how many decimal places are in the number and explain his or her answer. Have partners discuss the answer and help each other make corrections if necessary. Then have partners alternate roles and repeat the activity.

Using Grids to Multiply Decimals by Decimals

USE WITH LESSON 2-10

ACCESS CONTENT; EXTEND LANGUAGE

Objective Use grid models to find products of decimals.

Materials *(per student)* Decimal model for hundredths

ESL Strategies   *Use before* LEARN   ⏱ 5 MIN

Focus on Form ➤ Tell students that they will need to color tenths and hundredths to solve problems in this lesson. Write "tens" and "tenths" on the board. **How do these words look alike and different?** *(Both words have* ten *in them, but* tenths *has* th *before the* s.) **What are tens?** *(Tens are 10 ones)* **What are tenths?** *(Tenths are 10 parts of something, such as when you divide 1 into 10 equal parts.)* Repeat this line of questioning with *hundred* and *hundredths*.

Give each student a decimal model for hundredths. **How many tenths are there?** *(10)* **How many hundredths are there?** *(100)* **How many hundredths are in one tenth?** *(10)*

Use Manipulatives ➤ Write 0.3 on the board. Show students how they can show this number by shading 3 rows on a hundredths model. Write 0.2 on the board. **Shade this number in columns.** *(Check that students shade 2 columns on the hundredths model.)* **How did you solve the problem?** *(I shaded 3 rows, then I shaded 2 columns.)* Explain that where the shading overlaps is the solution. **There are 6 squares shaded, 6 hundredths.** Write 0.3 × 0.2 = 0.06 on the board.

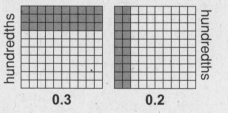

Multiplying Decimals by Decimals

USE WITH LESSON 2-11

ACTIVATE PRIOR KNOWLEDGE/BUILD BACKGROUND; ACCESS CONTENT

Objective Use partial products and the standard algorithm to multiply decimals by decimals.

Materials *(per pair)* 6-section spinner (Teaching Tool 9) labeled with numbers that have 0–3 decimal places.

Use before LEARN   ⏱ 10 MIN

How do you find the number of decimal places in a number? *(Count the number of digits to the right of the decimal point.)* Write 4.306 on the board. **How many decimal places are in this number? How do you know?** *(3 places; there are 3 digits to the right of the decimal point.)*

Write 1.52×4.3 vertically on the board. **How many decimal places are in 1.52?** *(2)* **How many decimal places are in 4.3?** *(1)* **If you add the decimal places in both numbers, how many decimal places do you have in all?** *(3)* Explain that when multiplying 1.52 and 4.3, 3 decimal places will appear in the product.

Divide the class into pairs. Have each partner spin the spinner and say or write the number of decimal places in his or her number. **How many decimal places do you have between the two of you?** *(Check that students add the number of decimal places in each number.)*

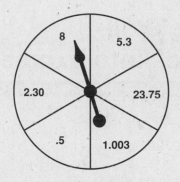

Variables and Expressions

EXTEND LANGUAGE; ACCESS CONTENT

Objective Use variables to write algebraic expressions.

Materials Index cards

Vocabulary Variable, algebraic expression

Use before LEARN   ⏱ 10 MIN

Write "<u>variable</u>" on the board. **A variable is a letter in a math statement that represents an amount or number.** Write $x + 4$, $2 - n$, and $a \times b$ on the board. **What are the variables in these expressions?** *(x, n, a, and b)*

What is an expression? *(A combination of numbers and mathematical symbols)* Write "<u>algebraic expression</u>." **An algebraic expression is a mathematical expression with at least one variable. What mathematical objects can be in an algebraic expression?** *(Numbers, variables, symbols)*

Assign students to groups of 4. Ask each student to write an algebraic expression on an index card. **Pass the card to the right. Is the expression algebraic? Explain.** When students have checked the expressions, have them pass the card to the right again. **Circle all of the variables and pass the card to the right.** Have students check that all the variables have been circled. Groups can repeat the activity several times to practice. Encourage students to explain aloud how they checked one another's answers.

Problem-Solving Skill: Translating Words into Expressions

USE WITH LESSON 2-13

ACTIVATE PRIOR KNOWLEDGE/BUILD BACKGROUND; ACCESS CONTENT

Objective Write number expressions for phrases.

Vocabulary Difference, product, quotient

ESL Strategies   *Use before* **LEARN**   ⏱ 10–15 MIN

Connect to Prior Knowledge of Math ➢ Write the symbols $+$, $-$, $\times$, and $\div$ on the board. As you point to each one, ask: **What operation does this symbol, or sign, tell us to use?** *(Addition, subtraction, multiplication, division)* Explain that symbols stand for these operations.

Use Demonstration ➢ Write "increased by 7" on the board. **What operation does the word *increased* tell us to use?** *(Addition)* Write "a <u>difference</u> of 21" on the board. **What operation does the word *difference* relate to?** *(Subtraction)* Explain that these words are clues that tell which operation is needed.

Name some other language cues for operations, such as *product*, *quotient*, *sum*, and *decreased*. As you read each word, have a volunteer write it on the board below the corresponding symbol. Help students understand that symbols and phrases often represent the same thing in mathematics.

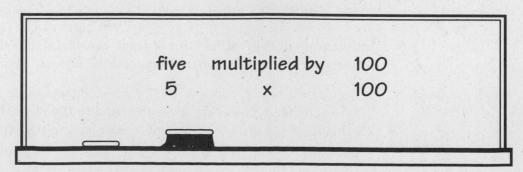

five	multiplied by	100
5	x	100

Algebra: Find a Rule

ACTIVATE PRIOR KNOWLEDGE/BUILD BACKGROUND; ACCESS CONTENT

Objective Identify patterns and find a rule for the pattern.

Materials Pairs of incomplete input/output tables using the same rule but with different examples (Teaching Tool 16)

Vocabulary Input/output table

ESL Strategies *Use before* CHECK ✓   ⏱ 10 MIN

Connect to Prior Knowledge of Math ➤ Refer to Student Book Page 106 to review how to find a rule for an <u>input/output table</u>. Explain that multiplying by the same number in each step is an example of a pattern. **What other kinds of rules have you seen that make patterns?** *(Sample answers: repeating numbers in the same order, adding the same number each time, subtracting the same number each time)*

Use Graphic Organizers ➤ Pass out input/output tables like the ones shown below. Write and explain the following directions.

> **1. Find a partner that has a table with the same rule. The table may have different numbers.**
>
> **2. Write the rule at the top of your table.**
>
> **3. Work together to finish both tables.**

Input	Output
2	4
3	6
6	
7	14

Input	Output
1	2
4	
	10
8	16

Solving Equations

ACCESS CONTENT

Objective Solve equations using mental mathematics and by guessing and testing values for the variable.

Materials *(per pair)* 20 pennies; 1 paper cup; 4 index cards

Vocabulary Equation

ESL Strategies *Use before* LEARN   ⏱ 10 MIN

Use Manipulatives ➤ Provide pairs of students with 20 pennies and a paper cup. Direct students to put the pennies on the desk between them. While one partner closes his or her eyes, the other partner hides some of the pennies in the cup. **How many pennies are left on the desk?** *(Sample answer: 17)* **We need to know how many pennies are missing from the desk. Let's call that number** *n.* **How many pennies should there be in all?** *(20)*

Show students how to write an <u>equation</u> to represent the model: $17 + n = 20$. Direct them to copy it on a card. **How many pennies are missing from the desk? Explain.** *(Sample answer: I think there are 3 pennies missing from the desk because 17 + 3 = 20.)* Have the partner who hid the pennies reveal how many pennies he or she put in the cup to confirm the answer. Tell students that in this exercise, *n* is equal to the number of pennies missing from the desk, or the number of pennies in the cup. Have each pair identify the number that *n* is equal to.

Give ➤
Frequent Feedback

Have partners take turns hiding the pennies and working together to writing and solving equations that represent the pennies. Check the work of each pair by asking students to explain what the values in their equations represent.

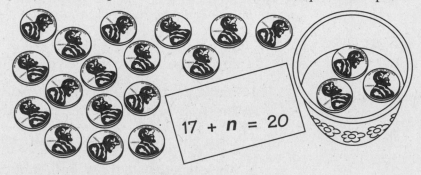

Problem-Solving Applications: Weight

USE WITH LESSON 2-16

ACTIVATE PRIOR KNOWLEDGE/BUILD BACKGROUND; ACCESS CONTENT

Objective Review and apply key concepts, skills, and strategies learned in this and previous chapters.

ESL Strategies

Use before **LEARN**

🕐 10 MIN

Use Small-Group ➤
Interactions

Write the following word problem on the board, excluding the answer, and then read it aloud.

> A perfume company sells a men's cologne in bottles that hold 3.4 fluid ounces. If the company ships 4 boxes that each hold 24 bottles of cologne, how many ounces are shipped altogether? If the cologne sells for $13.25 per ounce, what is the total retail value of each box? (326.4; $1,081.20)

Have students work in pairs to plan their strategies for solving the problem. Have them discuss and write down the steps they will use to answer each part of the problem. If any properties of multiliplication are used, have them identify these as well. Then ask each pair to compare its work with a neighboring pair and to decide whether both methods for finding the solution are valid.

The Meaning of Division

USE WITH LESSON 3-1

ACCESS CONTENT

Objective Draw a picture or use objects to show a division situation and find quotients.

Materials Two-color counters, paper, crayons

ESL Strategies | ***Use before*** **LEARN**   🕐 10 MIN

Use Manipulatives ➤ Distribute paper, crayons, and 12 counters to each student. **Draw 3 large circles on the paper. Put the same number of counters in each circle.** When students finish the activity, ask: **How many counters are in each circle?** *(4)* **Draw the counters in the circles to show what you did. What is 12 divided by 3?** *(4)* Write 12 ÷ 3 = 4 on the board and have students write it as a caption on the paper. Repeat the activity for 10 counters and 2 circles, 15 counters and 5 circles, 16 counters and 4 circles, and 12 counters and 2 circles.

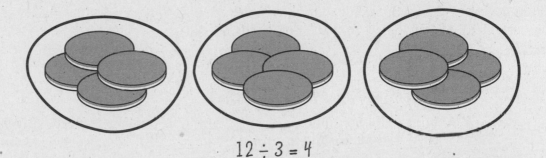

$$12 \div 3 = 4$$

Division Patterns

USE WITH LESSON 3-2

ACCESS CONTENT; EXTEND LANGUAGE

Objective Find the quotient of a division problem whose dividend is a multiple of 10, where the division involves a basic fact.

ESL Strategies | ***Use before*** **LEARN**   🕐 5 MIN

Use ➤ Demonstration **Basic division facts and patterns can help you solve more difficult division problems.** Write 24,000 ÷ 6 on the board. Cover the zeros in 24,000. **What is the quotient of 24 ÷ 6?** *(4)* **24 is the dividend. Which number is the divisor?** *(6)* **Suppose we multiply the dividend by 10.** Uncover one of the zeros. **What is the quotient of 240 ÷ 6? Explain.** *(40; The dividend 240 has one more zero in it than 24 and the divisor is the same, so the quotient has another zero.)* Repeat this step, uncovering one more zero each time until students solve 24,000 ÷ 6. Discuss the pattern and steps to solving 24,000 ÷ 6 with students. Use the terms *dividend, divisor,* and *quotient* as much as possible in the discussion.

Write 15,000 ÷ 3 on the board. Ask for a volunteer to explain the process of finding the quotient. Repeat the process with other volunteers and similar division problems.

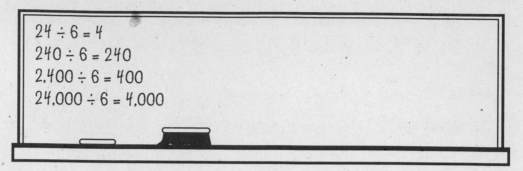

$24 \div 6 = 4$

$240 \div 6 = 240$

$2,400 \div 6 = 400$

$24,000 \div 6 = 4,000$

Estimating Quotients

USE WITH LESSON
3-3

ACTIVATE PRIOR KNOWLEDGE/BUILD BACKGROUND; ACCESS CONTENT

Objective Use rounding, compatible numbers, and multiplication to estimate quotients of whole numbers and money.

Materials 6 pink index cards with the numbers 5, 6, 7, 7, 8, 9; 6 yellow index cards with the numbers 120, 160, 2,000, 210, 27, 280

Vocabulary Compatible numbers

ESL Strategies

Use before CHECK ✓

⏱ 10 MIN

**Connect to Prior ➢
Knowledge of
Math**

Invite students to say "<u>compatible numbers</u>" after you. **What are compatible numbers?** *(Numbers that are easy to work with)* **In division, what are compatible numbers?** *(Numbers that are easy to divide mentally)*

**Use ➢
Peer Questioning**

Choose a volunteer and play one round of this game as a demonstration to the class. Then have students play in pairs.

Shuffle and place the cards facedown in a 3 × 4 grid, intermingling the pink and yellow cards. Have the first player draw one pink and one yellow card. Have the other player ask, "Are these compatible numbers?" Instruct the first player to respond, "Yes," or "No," and explain why or why not.

If both players agree that the numbers are compatible, the first player keeps the cards and the other player takes a turn. If not, the first player returns the cards to their starting locations and play passes to the other player. **The number on each card has a compatible number that's on another card. Keep playing until you've matched all the compatible numbers.**

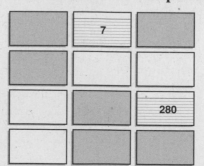

Problem-Solving Strategy: Look for a Pattern

USE WITH LESSON 3-4

ACCESS CONTENT

Objective Give missing numbers or figures in a pattern.

Materials Colored chalk; Power Polygons

ESL Strategies

Use before **LEARN**

⏱ 10 MIN

Use Pictures ➤ Display a pattern of figures that repeat the pattern unit *circle, square, triangle* four times. Ask students to describe what they see. Guide them to the understanding that the shapes repeat. **The shapes repeat to make a pattern.** Draw a pattern of circles that alternate colors. **Colors can also make a pattern.** Discuss the pattern with students. **What is a pattern?** *(A pattern is a set of objects that are repeated over and over.)*

Use Manipulatives ➤ Divide the class into small groups and give each group enough polygon figures to create their own patterns. Have students take turns creating patterns, while other students in the group identify each pattern and describe how it would continue. Encourage them to use the terms *pattern* and *repeat* in their explanations.

○○□○○□○○□

Understanding Division

USE WITH LESSON 3-5

ACCESS CONTENT; EXTEND LANGUAGE

Objective Find quotients using the model of sharing money.

Materials Bill Models (Teaching Tool 13)

ESL Strategies

Use before **LEARN**

⏱ 10 MIN

Use Manipulatives ➤ Give each group of 3 students $126 in the form of 1 hundred, 2 tens, and 6 ones. Set up a bank where students can exchange money such as hundreds for twenties or fives for ones. **Divide the $126 among the group so that you each have an equal amount.**

Have Students Report Back Orally ➤ When groups finish the activity, ask them to identify each student's share *($42)* and explain to the class how they solved the problem. Then put students into groups of 4 and repeat with $304, and into groups of 5 with $185.

Dividing Whole Numbers

USE WITH LESSON 3-6

ACCESS CONTENT; EXTEND LANGUAGE

Objective Divide three-digit whole numbers by one-digit divisors.

Vocabulary Dividend, divisor

ESL Strategies

Use before **LEARN**

⏱ 10 MIN

Use Demonstration ➤ Write $427 \div 7$ and $7\overline{)427}$ on the board. **What is a <u>dividend</u>?** *(The number being divided in a division problem)* Point to the first problem. **Which number is the dividend?** *(427)* **How many digits does it have?** *(3)* **What is a <u>divisor</u>?** *(The number divided into the dividend)* **Which number is the divisor?** *(7)* **How many digits does it have?** *(1)* Point to the second problem. **When a problem is written this way, where is the dividend? The divisor?** *(Under the division house; to the left)*

Write the problem $3\overline{)732}$ on the left and $8\overline{)432}$ on the right. Explain that students will learn to solve problems dividing 3-digit dividends by 1-digit divisors. **The first step is to decide where to place the first digit in the quotient.** Point to the 3 in the first problem. **Is 3 less than 7?** *(Yes)* **Then the first digit in the quotient goes above the 7.** Write the answer 243. Point to the 8 in the second problem. **Is 8 less than 4?** *(No)* **Then the first digit in the quotient goes above the next number.** Write the answer 54 so that the 5 is above the 3 in 432.

Have Students Report Back Orally ➤ Assign each student a division problem with a 3-digit number divided by a 1-digit divisor, such as $564 \div 6$. Have each student rewrite the problem with a division house, decide where to place the first digit of the quotient, and then mark the position with an x. Ask each student to present his or her work on the board and explain the answer to a small group or the class.

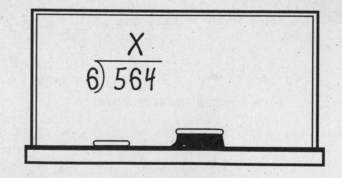

Zeros in the Quotient

ACCESS CONTENT

Objective Divide with zeros in the quotient.

Materials Place-value models; place-value charts

ESL Strategies **Use before** **LEARN** ⏱ 5 MIN

Use Manipulatives ➤ Give 4 hundreds models and 12 ones models to a group of four volunteers. **Can we divide these counting materials evenly between these four students?** Divide the total number of models used to make 412 equally among the students. Remind students that they may need to regroup hundreds or tens. **Now each student should have an equal number of hundreds, tens, and ones.**

Use Graphic ➤ Have students copy and complete a place-value chart to show how many
Organizers hundreds, tens, and ones each person has. **How many hundreds, tens, and ones do you have?** *(1, 0, 3)* **So, what is 412 ÷ 4?** *(103)* **Why is there a zero in your answer?** *(I don't have any tens.)*

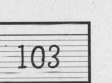

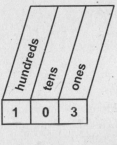

Dividing Larger Dividends

ACTIVATE PRIOR KNOWLEDGE/BUILD BACKGROUND

Objective Find the quotients of 4-digit whole numbers divided by 1-digit divisors.

ESL Strategies **Use before** **LEARN** ⏱ 5–10 MIN

Connect to Prior ➤ Write 5)4,957 on the board. **How many digits are in the dividend? In the**
Knowledge of **divisor?** *(4; 1)* **How is this problem like a 3-digit number divided by a 1-**
Math **digit divisor?** *(Both problems have 1-digit divisors.)* **How is it different?** *(The dividend has 4 digits rather than 3 digits.)* Point to the divisor 5. **Will the first digit in the quotient be placed above the 4 or the 9 in 4,957? How do you know?** *(It will be above the 9. Since the divisor 5 is greater than the first digit in the dividend, 4, the first digit in the quotient goes above the second digit.)* Ask students to explain how they think dividing a 4-digit number by a 1-digit divisor will be alike and different than working with a 3-digit dividend. *(Sample answer: The kinds of steps will be the same but there may be more steps to get to the answer.)*

Dieviving Money

ACCESS CONTENT

USE WITH LESSON 3-9

Objective Find quotients of money amounts divided by one-digit divisors.

Materials Bill and Coin Models (Teaching Tool 13)

ESL Strategies **Use before** **LEARN** ⏱ 5 MIN

Use Manipulatives ➤ Have groups of three students model $9.72 with bills and coins, then divide the money equally among them. Remind students that they may have to regroup. **How much money does each student have?** *($3.24)* **What is $9.72 ÷ 3?** *($3.24)*

Use Demonstration ➤ On the board, write and explain the long-division steps for 972 ÷ 3 and $9.72 ÷ 3 side by side. **How are the two problems alike?** *(You follow the same steps to solve each problem.)* **How are they different?** Encourage students to use the term *decimal point* in their responses. *(Sample answer: One problem has a decimal point and the other doesn't. You have to put the decimal point in the right place in the answer when you divide money.)*

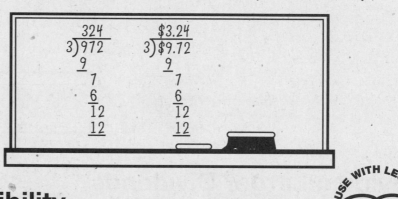

Factors and Divisibility

ACCESS CONTENT; EXTEND LANGUAGE

USE WITH LESSON 3-10

Objective Determine if numbers are divisible by 2, 3, 4, 5, 6, 9, or 10.

Materials Place-Value Models (Teaching Tool 1)

Vocabulary Divisible

ESL Strategies **Use before** **LEARN** ⏱ 10 MIN

Use Manipulatives ➤ Make a two-column chart headed by "Divisible by 4" and "Not divisible by 4." Write the numbers 12, 16, 20, and 24 in the first column and 13, 15, 18, and 21 in the second column. **Let's find out what it means for a number to be <u>divisible</u> by 4.** Point to the word *divisible* as you say it. **Model 12 and divide it into groups of 4. Are there any left over?** *(No)* Write 12 ÷ 4 = 3 on the board. Repeat for 16, 20, and 24. **What do these quotients have in common?** *(There is no remainder.)* **Now model 13 and divide it into groups of 4. Are there any left over?** *(Yes; there is one left over)* Write 13 ÷ 4 = 3R1 on the board. Repeat for 15, 18, and 21. **What do all of these quotients have in common?** *(They have a remainder.)*

Focus on Meaning ➤ **What does it mean for a number to be divisible by 4?** *(It can be divided by 4 without a remainder.)* **What does it mean if a number is not divisible by 4?** *(If it is divided by 4, there is a remainder.)* **What does if mean if a number is divisible by 9?** *(If you divide the number by 9, there will be no remainder.)* **Is 15 divisible by 3? Explain.** *(Yes; If you divide 15 ÷ 3, there is no remainder.)*

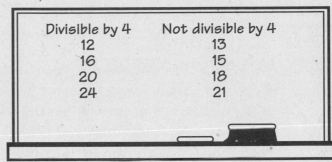

Divisible by 4	Not divisible by 4
12	13
16	15
20	18
24	21

Prime and Composite Numbers

USE WITH LESSON **3-11**

ACTIVATE PRIOR KNOWLEDGE/BUILD BACKGROUND; ACCESS CONTENT

Objective Identify numbers as prime or composite.

Materials Number Cards for 2, 3, 4, 7, 8, and 10 (Teaching Tool 8)

Vocabulary Prime number, composite number

ESL Strategies | *Use before* **LEARN** | ⏱ 10 MIN

Use Graphic Organizers ➤ Review the meaning of the word *factor*.

Write the numbers 2, 3, 4, 7, 8, 10 in a vertical column on the board. Have a volunteer come to the board and write the factors of 2 next to that number. Have different volunteers repeat the activity for the remaining numbers until the table is filled in. **What do you notice about the numbers 2, 3, and 7?** *(They only have 2 factors.)* **What does each pair of factors have in common?** *(In each pair, the factors are the number itself and 1.)* **Numbers that have only 2 factors are called <u>prime numbers</u>. Numbers that have more than 2 factors are called <u>composite numbers</u>. Which of these are composite numbers?** *(4, 8, 10)* Point to the composite numbers.

Use Manipulatives ➤ Write several numbers on the board and help students determine whether each is prime or composite. **Is 6 prime or composite? How do you know?** *(Composite; it has 4 factors—1, 2, 3, and 6.)* **Is 5 prime or composite? How do you know?** *(Prime; it has only 2 factors—1 and 5.)*

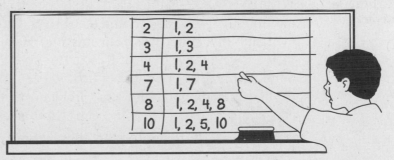

2	1, 2
3	1, 3
4	1, 2, 4
7	1, 7
8	1, 2, 4, 8
10	1, 2, 5, 10

Problem-Solving Skill: Interpreting Remainders

USE WITH LESSON 3-12

ACTIVATE PRIOR KNOWLEDGE/BUILD BACKGROUND; ACCESS CONTENT

Objective Interpret remainders by giving total amounts needed to include remainders, and amounts left over.

Materials 3 desks, 8 chairs

ESL Strategies

Use before LEARN

⏱ 10 MIN

Use Simulation ➤ Set up 2 small desks or tables with 3 chairs at each. Tell students that a new restaurant has just opened, and a lot of people want to eat there. Have 9 volunteers come to the front of the room; have 8 of them act as customers and the other one act as the waiter. **At this restaurant, only three people can sit at each table.** Have the waiter seat the customers in the chairs until they are full. **How many tables are full?** *(2 tables)* **How many people remain, or are left over?** *(2 people)* **What will we need for them?** *(A new table)* Have the waiter set up a third table and chairs for the remaining 2 customers. **How many tables did you need in all?** *(3)*

Paraphrase Ideas ➤ Write 8 ÷ 3 = 2 R2 on the board. **What is the quotient?** *(2 R2)* **Why do we use a remainder in the quotient?** *(3 does not divide into 8 evenly.)* **Why did the waiter add a third table?** *(The extra people needed a table.)*

Order of Operations

USE WITH LESSON 3-13

ACCESS CONTENT

Objective Evaluate expressions with three or more numbers and two or more operations.

ESL Strategies

Use before LEARN

⏱ 5 MIN

Use Small-Group Interactions ➤ Write 3 + 4 × 2 on the board. Assign students partners. Have one partner multiply first, then add to find the answer. Have the other partner add first, then multiply. **What was your answer?** Have students compare and explain their answers to each other. Repeat for 10 − 2 × 3, having one student multiply first and one subtract first. Repeat for 6 + 9 ÷ 3. Guide students to the understanding that the same problem can have different answers depending on the order of the steps. **In this lesson, you will learn the proper order of those steps so that you always get the right answer.**

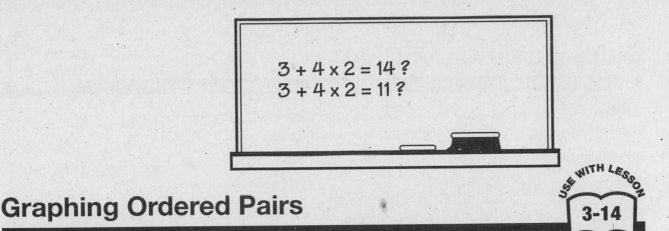

Graphing Ordered Pairs

ACCESS CONTENT

Objective On a coordinate grid, plot points for ordered pairs and identify the ordered pairs for plotted points.

Materials Centimeter Grid Paper (Teaching Tool 49)

ESL Strategies *Use before* **LEARN**   10 MIN

Use Gestures ➤ Distribute a grid to each student and display a large grid for the class. **There are two lines, or axes, that are the main parts of a grid.** Identify the *x*-axis by tracing it with your finger and labeling it with the letter *x*. Have students mimic your actions of tracing and labeling on their grids. Explain that the *x*-axis is the horizontal or side-to-side axis.

Repeat the activity with the *y*-axis. Explain that the *y*-axis is the vertical or up-and-down axis. Point to the origin. **This is called the *origin*. How would you describe the origin?** *(The place where the x-axis and y-axis meet)*

Use Small-Group Interactions ➤ Have students work together in small groups to devise ways to remember which is the *x*-axis and which is the *y*-axis. Example: The letter *y* has a long, vertical tail, so it describes the up/down axis. Have groups share their ideas with the class.

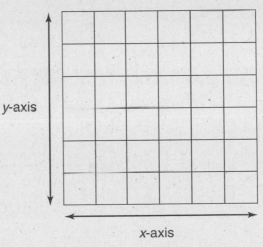

Rules, Tables, and Graphs

ACTIVATE PRIOR KNOWLEDGE/BUILD BACKGROUND; EXTEND LANGUAGE

Objective Create a table of values for a rule and a graph based on the table, and use the table or graph to give the output for an input.

Materials Input/Output Tables (Teaching Tool 16)

Vocabulary Table of values

ESL Strategies   *Use before* CHECK ✓   🕐 10–15 MIN

Connect to Prior ➤
Knowledge of
Math

What is a rule in math? *(A sentence or expression that tells you which operations to perform)* Write $10n + 2$ on the board. **This is an example of an algebraic rule.** Give students the opportunity to discuss what this means. **For each number I put in for *n* I multiply it by 10 and add 2 to the result. What is the result if *n* is 3?** *(32)* **What steps did you take to find the answer?** *(10 \times 3 = 30; 30 + 2 = 32)*

Have Students ➤
Report Back
Orally

Have students work in pairs. Have one partner from each pair write an algebraic rule on a piece of paper. Have the other partner describe what it means in words. Direct partners to work together to write five pairs of numbers on a table of values using that rule. To get students started, you might want to model how to complete a table of values for an algebraic rule. Suggest that students try using 1–5 as the input numbers. Then have them take turns describing the steps they followed in order to use the rule on each set of numbers.

$$2x + 3$$

1	5
2	7
3	9
4	11
5	13

Problem-Solving Applications: High Speed Trains

ACCESS CONTENT

Objective Review and apply key concepts, skills, and strategies learned in this and previous chapters.

ESL Strategies

Use before **LEARN** ⏱ 10 MIN

Use Small-Group ➤ Interactions

Write the following word problem on the board, excluding the answer, and then read it aloud.

> An inter-city high speed train has an average cruising speed of 211 kilometers per hour. To the nearest whole kilometer, how far can it travel in half an hour? In 15 minutes? (*106 km; 53 km*)

Have students work in pairs to solve the problem. You might suggest that they describe in writing what the problem is asking. If necessary, prompt them to make a table like the one below to help them solve it.

Then ask each pair to compare with a neighboring pair their method of interpreting the remainder. (*Possible answers: For the distance in $\frac{1}{2}$ h, the remainder is half of the divisor, so I rounded up. For the distance in $\frac{1}{4}$ h, the remainder is more than half the divisor so I rounded up.*)

Speed	211	211	211
Time	1	$\frac{1}{2}$ hour	$\frac{1}{4}$ hour
Compute	$211 \div 1 = 211$	$211 \div 2 = 105$	$211 \div 4 = 52$
		R1	R3

Dividing by Multiples of 10

ACCESS CONTENT; ACTIVATE PRIOR KNOWLEDGE/BUILD BACKGROUND

Objective Find the quotients of division problems whose dividends and divisors are multiples of 10, where the division involves a basic fact.

Vocabulary Multiple of 10

ESL Strategies   *Use before*   **LEARN**   ⏲ 10 MIN

Use Graphic Organizers ➤ Write 10, 100, 1,000, and 10,000 in a column on the board, aligning the digit 1 in each number. **What do all of these numbers have in common?** *(They begin with the number 1 followed by zeros.)* **How are the numbers different?** *(Each number has a different number of zeros.)* **What pattern do you see?** *(Each number has one more zero than the number before it.)*

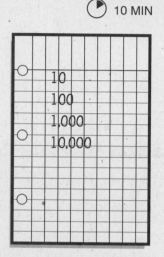

Connect to Prior Knowledge of Math ➤ Focus students' attention on the numbers 10 and 100. **What number do you multiply by 10 to get 100?** *(10)* Direct students' attention to 100 and 1,000. **What number do you multiply by 100 to get 1,000?** *(10)* Repeat for 1,000 and 10,000. **The word *multiple* comes from *multiply*. Why do you think the numbers in this chart are called <u>multiples of 10</u>?** *(Sample answer: You multiply by 10 to get each number in the chart.)* Guide students to the meaning of *multiples of 10*. Explain that they will learn to divide by multiples of 10 in this lesson.

Estimating with Two-Digit Divisors

ACTIVATE PRIOR KNOWLEDGE/BUILD BACKGROUND; ACCESS CONTENT

Objective Estimate quotients with whole numbers, decimals, and money divided by two-digit whole numbers.

Vocabulary Compatible numbers

ESL Strategies   *Use before*   **LEARN**   ⏲ 10 MIN

Connect to Prior Knowledge of Math ➤ Remind students that they have used <u>compatible numbers</u> to estimate answers in division problems. **What are compatible numbers in division?** *(Two numbers that are easy to divide using mental math.)* **Are 120 and 4 compatible numbers?** *(Yes)* **Are 120 and 40 compatible numbers?** *(Yes)* **How do you know?** *(120 and 40 are multiples of 12 and 4. It is easy to divide 12 ÷ 4.)*

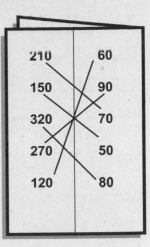

Use Small-Group Interactions ➤ Divide the class into pairs. Have students fold a sheet of paper in half vertically and draw a line down the middle. Have them write the numbers 210, 150, 320, 270, and 120 down the left side and the numbers 60, 90, 70, 50, and 80 down the right side. Have one partner identify a pair of compatible numbers, choosing one number from each column. He or she should then explain the reasoning behind his or her choice. (*I think 150 and 50 are compatible numbers because 15 divides easily by 5.*) If the other partner agrees, they draw a line to connect the numbers. Students take turns finding a pair of compatible numbers until all of the matches are made.

Problem-Solving Strategy: Try, Check, and Revise

USE WITH LESSON 4-3

ACTIVATE PRIOR KNOWLEDGE/BUILD BACKGROUND; EXTEND LANGUAGE

Objective Solve problems using the *Try, Check, and Revise* strategy.

ESL Strategies **Use before** **LEARN**   ⏱ 10 MIN

Explain that a useful strategy for solving problems is called *Try, Check, and Revise.* **Let's look at each word in this strategy to figure out what it means.** Ask students to tell short stories about when they have tried to do something. **What does *try* mean?** (*Sample answers: Take a chance, give a go, take a shot, attempt*)

In math, you often check your answers. Name other times when you check something. (*Sample answer: I look outside to check if it is raining.*) **What does check mean?** (*Sample answers: Make sure, confirm, test, prove, assess*)

Revise **means to correct, improve, or change something. What does it mean if I revise an estimate of the number of apples in a basket?** (*It means you change your estimate to make it better or more accurate.*)

Have students write "1. Try 2. Check 3. Revise" on a sheet of paper. Write the three steps in your own words using a synonym for each term. Encourage students with very limited English skills to use their native languages as necessary. Have students share their definitions with partners or small groups.

1. Guess.

2. Test.

3. Improve.

Dividing Whole Numbers by Two-Digit Divisors

USE WITH LESSON 4-4

ACTIVATE PRIOR KNOWLEDGE/BUILD BACKGROUND; ACCESS CONTENT

Objective Use the standard algorithm to divide three-digit whole numbers by two-digit divisors.

ESL Strategies · *Use before* LEARN · ⏱ 5–10 MIN

Connect to Prior Knowledge of Math ➤ **What is a divisor?** *(The number that you divide by)* Write $432 \div 6 = 72$ on the board. **Which number is the divisor?** *(6)* **How do you know?** *(It is the number by which you are dividing 432.)* Write $9)\overline{216}$ with 24 above on the board. **Which number is the divisor?** *(9)*

Use Graphic Organizers ➤ Write $6)\overline{432}$ and $48)\overline{432}$ side by side on the board. **How are these problems alike?** *(They have the same dividend, or the number that is being divided.)* **How are they different?** *(They have different divisors.)* **How are the divisors different?** *(6 is a one-digit divisor, but 48 is a two-digit divisor.)* **How might dividing by 48 be different from dividing by 6?** *(Sample answer: The steps will be the same, but you will have to be careful where to place the first digit in the quotient.)* **You can divide 43 by 6, so the first digit in the quotient goes above the 3. You cannot divide 43 by 48, however. So the first digit in that quotient goes above the 2.** Tell students that in this lesson, they will use what they know about dividing by one-digit divisors to divide by two-digit divisors.

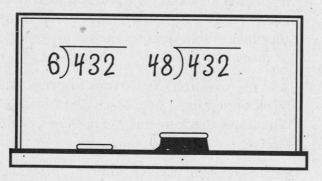

Dividing Larger Numbers

USE WITH LESSON 4-5

ACCESS CONTENT; EXTEND LANGUAGE

Objective Use the standard algorithm to find the quotient of four-digit whole numbers divided by two-digit divisors.

Materials *(per pair)* 2 index cards

ESL Strategies · *Use before* LEARN · ⏱ 10 MIN

Use Small-Group Interactions ➤ Write $1{,}792 \div 16$ on the board. **How many digits are in the dividend of this problem?** *(Four)* **How many digits are in the divisor?** *(Two)*

In this lesson, you will learn how to divide a four-digit dividend by a two-digit divisor. Divide the class into pairs. Have each partner write a division problem with a four-digit dividend and a two-digit divisor on an index card. Then ask partners to trade cards. **How many digits are in the dividend?** *(Four)* **The divisor?** *(Two)* Then have partners work together to come up with a plan for solving the problems.

Have Students Report Back Orally ➤ Ask partners to present their strategy for solving one of their division problems.

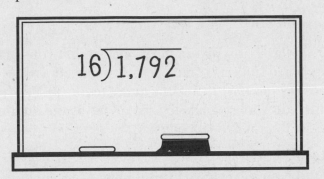

Dividing:
Choose a Computation Method

USE WITH LESSON 4-6

ACCESS CONTENT

Objective For a variety of problems, state the computation method to be used and divide using that method.

Materials *(per pair)* Place-value models; calculator

ESL Strategies | **Use before** LEARN | 🕐 10–15 MIN

Use Manipulatives ➤ Write the following word problem on the board: "You have 96 eggs. There are 12 eggs in a dozen. How many dozen eggs do you have?" *(8 dozen)* Distribute place-value models to pairs of students. Have one partner solve the problem using the models, then record his or her answer.

Write this problem on the board: "You read 126 pages in 6 weeks. How many pages did you read each week?" *(21 pages)* Have the other partner use the models to solve this problem and record his or her answer. Then distribute a calculator to each pair and have each partner check the other's work. **Did you get the same answers? Was it easier to work with the models or the calculator?** *(Accept responses students can justify.)* Change the numbers in the second problem on the board so that it states "You read 100 pages in 2 weeks." **What method would you use to solve this problem now? Would you use models, a calculator, or would you try to solve the problem in your head?** *(Accept responses students can justify.)*

Dividing with Zeros in the Quotient

ACCESS CONTENT

Objective Divide numbers whose quotients include zeros.

Materials *(per group)* Place-value models

 ESL Strategies

Use before **LEARN**

🕐 10 MIN

Use Manipulatives ➤ Have groups of 3 students model 618 using place-value models. Write 618 ÷ 3 on the board. **Divide the model so that you each have the same amount.** When students complete the assignment, ask: **How many hundreds do you have?** *(2)* **How many tens?** *(0)* **How many ones?** *(6)* **How much do you each have?** *(206)* **What is the quotient of 618 ÷ 3?** *(206)* Write the answer on the board.

Repeat the activity for 309 ÷ 3 *(103)*, 60 ÷ 3 *(20)*, and 921 ÷ 3 *(307)*. **What do all of the quotients have in common?** *(They have a zero.)* **Why do we write the zero in the quotient if it stands for nothing? Why can't we just write the answers as 26, 13, 2, and 37?** *(The zero in the quotient holds a place in the number; without the zero, the value of the number changes.)* Explain that students will learn the steps to divide numbers with zeros in the quotient.

$12

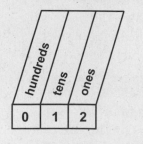

hundreds	tens	ones
0	1	2

$102

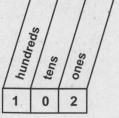

hundreds	tens	ones
1	0	2

Problem-Solving Skill: Multiple-Step Problems

USE WITH LESSON
4-8

EXTEND LANGUAGE; ACCESS CONTENT

Objective Solve multiple-step word problems.

Materials *(per child)* Coin Models (Teaching Tool 13)

ESL Strategies *Use before* **LEARN** ⏱ 10 MIN

Focus on Meaning ➤ **What do you think *multiple* means?** *(Many, more than one)* **What do you think a multiple-step problem is?** *(A problem with more than one step)* Explain that in some problems, one step has to be solved before the next step can be performed.

Use Manipulatives ➤ Write the problem shown in the illustration below on the board. **What do you need to do first to solve this problem?** *(You need to add 50¢ and 32¢ to find the total amount Diego spent.)* Ask students to use coin models or make a drawing to show this step. **How much did Diego spend in all?** *(Diego spent 82¢.)* **What do you need to do next to solve this problem?** *(You need to find the difference between 82¢ and $1.00 to find the change.)* **What is the difference?** *(18¢)* **How much change did Diego receive?** *(18¢)*

Use Small-Group Interactions ➤ Divide the class into groups. Give the groups similar problems to solve using the coin models. Have one student in the group record the steps as they proceed. Encourage students to discuss their steps with other groups.

> Diego bought an apple for 50¢ and a banana for 32¢. He paid with a one-dollar bill. How much change did he receive?

Dividing Decimals by 10, 100, and 1,000

USE WITH LESSON
4-9

ACCESS CONTENT

Objective Divide decimal numbers by 10, 100, and 1,000.

ESL Strategies *Use before* **LEARN** ⏱ 5 MIN

Use Graphic Organizers ➤ Draw a two-column chart on the board. **What is 635 ÷ 1?** *(635.0)* Have a volunteer find the answer. Have a second volunteer write the number 1 in the first column and the answer in the second column. Instruct this student to include the decimal point in the answer. **What is 635 ÷ 10?** *(63.5)* Again

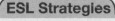

have a volunteer find the answer. Then have another volunteer write the divisor and the answer on the board. Have different students complete the chart on the board so that the first column contains 1, 10, 100, and 1,000 and the second column contains 635.0, 63.5, 6.35, and 0.635. **How many zeros are in 10?** *(1 zero)* **When you divide a number by 10, what do you do with the decimal point?** *(You move the decimal point one place to the left in the number. That number is then the quotient.)* Repeat this line of questioning for dividing by 100 and 1,000. **What does the number of zeros in these divisors tell you to do with the decimal point?** *(Move the decimal point that many places to the left.)*

Dividing Money by Two-Digit Divisors

USE WITH LESSON 4-10

ACCESS CONTENT

Objective Use the standard algorithm to find quotients of money amounts divided by two-digit divisors.

Materials *(per child)* Coin Models (Teaching Tool 13)

ESL Strategies   *Use before* **LEARN**   🕐 10–15 MIN

Use Manipulatives ➤ Write 75¢ ÷ 5 on the board. Have students model the problem with coin models. **What is 75¢ ÷ 5?** *(15¢)* Write 75¢ ÷ 25 on the board. **How are the two problems alike?** *(You divide a money amount.)* **How are they different?** *(One has a one-digit divisor and the other has a two-digit divisor.)* **Can you divide 7 by 25?** *(No)* **Can you divide 75 by 25?** *(Yes)* **How will the quotient be different than in the first problem?** *(The quotient will only be one digit.)* Repeat the activity with different money amounts. **In this lesson, you will learn to divide money amounts by two-digit divisors.**

Dividing Decimals by Whole Numbers

ACCESS CONTENT

Objective Use the standard algorithm to find the quotient of two- and three-digit decimal numbers divided by two-digit divisors.

ESL Strategies | ***Use before*** **CHECK ✓** | ⏱ 10 MIN

Use Graphic Organizers ➤ Have students make a flowchart like the one shown below. Be sure students make their rectangles large enough to write in. Write the following four steps and instruct students to copy them into their flowchart in the proper order.

> Divide the ones. *(Step 1)*
>
> Divide the tenths. *(Step 2)*
>
> Divide the hundredths. *(Step 3)*
>
> Check by multiplying. *(Step 4)*

Use Small-Group Interactions ➤ Divide the class into pairs. Write 3.22 ÷ 7 and 4.52 ÷ 4 on the board. Have each partner select a problem and use the flowchart to help him or her solve it. Partners then take turns demonstrating their solutions to each other. Encourage each student to check his or her partner's answer and to ask questions about the steps he or she took to solve the problem. *(0.46, 1.13)*

Problem-Solving Applications: Animal Speeds

ACCESS CONTENT

Objective Review and apply key concepts, skills, and strategies learned in this and previous chapters.

ESL Strategies | ***Use before*** **LEARN** | ⏱ 10 MIN

Use Small-Group Interactions ➤ Write the following word problem on the board, excluding the answer, and then read it aloud.

> "A three-toed sloth moves at an average speed of 0.15 miles per hour. A giant tortoise moves at an average speed of 0.17 miles per hour. Which animal covers a greater distance, the sloth in 15 minutes or the tortoise in 12 minutes?" *(The sloth in 15 min covers 0.0375 mi, but the tortoise in 12 minutes only covers 0.034 mi.)*

Have students work in pairs to write division sentences that will help them solve the problem. Also, have them discuss and write down any hidden information in the problem. *(To find the distance covered in 15 minutes, or $\frac{1}{4}$ hour, divide by 4; to find the distance covered in 12 minutes, or $\frac{1}{5}$ hour, divide by 5.)* Then ask volunteers from several pairs to describe their strategy for solving the problem.

Collecting Data from a Survey

EXTEND LANGUAGE; ACCESS CONTENT

Objective Identify a statement as fact or opinion. Interpret a line plot and a frequency table. Write a survey question.

Materials Colored chalk

Vocabulary Survey

ESL Strategies | *Use before* **LEARN** | 🕐 10 MIN

Focus on Meaning ➤ **What does the word** *fact* **mean?** *(Information that is true)* Have students state some facts about things around them such as color of objects. **What is an opinion?** *(Information that tells what someone thinks about something)* Have students state some opinions about things around them, such as their favorite colors.

Use Graphic ➤ Ask several students to name their favorite fruits. Write their responses on
Organizers the board. **I have just taken a** <u>survey</u>. Draw word webs like the ones shown below. Write the words "question" and "answer" in different colors of chalk. Point to the web on the left. **This diagram shows that 1 person gave an answer to a question. Point to the other web. What does this diagram show?** *(Many people gave answers to the same question.)* Write the word "survey" over the word web on the right. **A survey is when you ask many people the same question and record, or write down, their answers. In this lesson, you will learn more about how to collect information using a survey.**

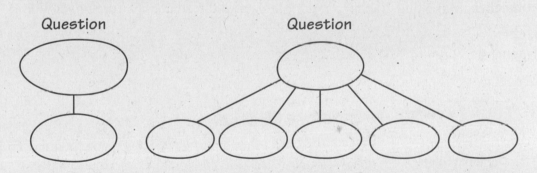

Bar Graphs

ACCESS CONTENT; ACTIVATE PRIOR KNOWLEDGE/BUILD BACKGROUND

Objective Make double bar graphs to represent data.

Materials 1 rectangular object such as a board eraser

Use before LEARN

🕐 10 MIN

Use Demonstration ➤ Draw a set of vertical and horizontal axes on the board. Number the vertical axis from 0-30 (or more for a bigger class size) in increments of 2. Label the vertical axis "Number of Students." Have students with blue eyes raise their hands. Call on a volunteer to count the number of raised hands. Draw a bar of this height on the graph. Repeat for brown eyes and any other eye colors in the class. Label each bar with the appropriate eye color on the horizontal axis. **This bar graph makes it easy for us to compare the numbers.** Extend the horizontal axis. Guide volunteers in using the same process to construct bars for hair color. Help them to label each bar correctly.

Connect to Prior Knowledge of Language ➤ Point to the bars in the graph. **What shape is this?** *(Rectangle)* Relate the words *bar* and *rectangle* with a familiar object such as a board eraser. **We can show different numbers on the bar graph with rectangles of different lengths.**

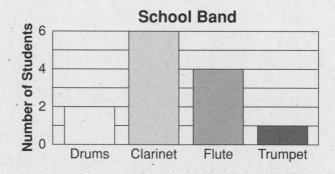

Line Graphs

ACCESS CONTENT; EXTEND LANGUAGE

USE WITH LESSON
5-3

Objective Make line graphs to represent data, and read and interpret given line graphs.

Materials *(per pair)* At least 1 magazine or newspaper

Vocabulary Line graph

Use before LEARN

🕐 10 MIN

Use Demonstration ➤ Draw a set of vertical and horizontal axes on the board. Label the vertical axis "Inches of Snow" and the horizontal axis "Hours." Draw a straight line to show that 1 in. fell every hour. **This line graph shows the amount of snow that fell during a storm. Why do you think we call it a *line graph*?** *(We show*

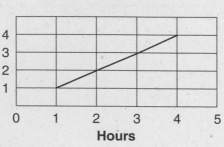

the information with a line.) Point to the "1 hour" mark on the horizontal axis. **How much snow fell in 1 hour?** *(1 inch)* Show students how to read this information from the graph. Repeat for other points on the graph.

Have Students ➤ Report Back Orally

Have pairs of students search magazines or newspapers to find an example of a line graph. Guide the pairs to determine what kind of information the graph shows. Have pairs explain to the class what their graphs mean. Repeat with several pairs of students. If students cannot find a line graph in a magazine or newspaper, invite them to make their own. Help students label their line graphs and determine increments of measure as needed.

Stem-and-Leaf Plots

USE WITH LESSON 5-4

ACTIVATE PRIOR KNOWLEDGE/BUILD BACKGROUND; ACCESS CONTENT

Objective Complete, make, and interpret stem-and-leaf plots.

Materials *(per student)* 1 sheet of paper; 1 pencil

Vocabulary Stem, leaf, stem-and-leaf plot

ESL Strategies   *Use before*   **LEARN**   ⏱ 10 MIN

Connect to Prior ➤ Experiences

Show a picture of a tree or plant and discuss with students the location and relationship of the <u>stems</u> and <u>leaves</u>. Help them realize that each stem supports, or holds, many leaves.

Use Pictures ➤

Display a <u>stem-and-leaf plot</u> similar to the one on Student Book Page 270. **This kind of graph is called a *stem-and-leaf plot.*** Identify the stem and leaf portions of the diagram. **In what ways does the graph look like the picture?** Guide students to understand that there are support stems on the left and a number of leaves for each stem on the right.

Stem	Leaf
6	2 3 6
7	1 8
8	3 5 7 8 9
9	2 2 4 5 9 9

Use ➤ Demonstration

Have students get out a sheet of paper and a pencil. **Now we will make our own stem-and-leaf plot. We will use our stem-and-leaf plot to organize numbers.** List the following numbers on the board: 20, 27, 51, 43, 31, 10, 15, 19, 30, 50, 42. **We will put these numbers in order from least to greatest using a stem-and-leaf plot.** Draw 2 columns on the board with the headings "stem" and "leaf." Have students do the same on their papers. List the numbers 1–5 under the stem column and have students do the same. **These stems show the first digit in our list of numbers.** Point to 1 in the stem column. **Which numbers in our list start with this digit?** *(10, 15, 19)* **We will write the second digit for these numbers in order from least to greatest in the leaf column.** Write 0 5 9 in the leaf column next to the first stem. Have students write this in their stem-and-leaf plots. Continue the activity, asking students what numbers will be recorded for each stem. Have volunteers tell what will be written in the leaf column. Complete the stem-and-leaf plot on the board while students complete the plot on their papers.

Problem-Solving Strategy: Make a Graph

USE WITH LESSON 5-5

ACTIVATE PRIOR KNOWLEDGE/BUILD BACKGROUND; ACCESS CONTENT

Objective Make a line plot and a double bar graph to solve problems.

Materials *(per student)* 1 sheet of paper; 1 pencil

ESL Strategies | **Use before** LEARN | ⏱ 10 MIN

Connect to Prior Knowledge of Math ➤ Have students use their textbooks to list the 3 kinds of graphs they have learned about in this chapter. **What are the names of the 3 kinds of graphs?** *(Double bar graph, line graph, stem-and-leaf plot)*

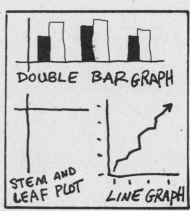

Use Pictures ➤ Have students sketch and label each kind of graph. **What can a line graph be used for?** *(To show how something changes over time)* **What does a double bar graph show?** *(Rectangular bars that compare data)* **How does a stem-and-leaf plot show data?** *(Uses 2 columns to organize the numbers)*

Mean, Median, and Mode

USE WITH LESSON 5-6

EXTEND LANGUAGE; ACCESS CONTENT

Objective Find the mean, median, mode, and range of a set of data, and choose the measure that best represents a given set of data.

Materials Index cards

Vocabulary Mean, median, mode

ESL Strategies | **Use before** CHECK ✓ | ⏱ 15 MIN

Focus on Meaning ➤ Write 9, 10, 11, 12, 14, 16, 17, 17, 17, 18, 24 on the board. **In this lesson, we will learn how to analyze data using the mean, median, mode, and range.** Write the following statements on the board: "mean = average," "median = middle," "mode = most," "range = greatest minus least." **How do you find the mean?** *(Find the average of all the numbers.)* **How do you find the** average of all the numbers? *(Add all the numbers together. Divide the sum by the total amount of numbers.)* **Find the mean for these numbers.** *(15)* Calculate the mean together with students. Write the average on the board. **How do you find the median?** *(Find the middle number.)* **Find the median.** *(16)* Underline the median on the board. **How do you find the mode?** *(Find the most common number.)* **Find the mode.** *(17)* Circle the mode on the board. **How do you find the range?** *(Find the difference between the least and greatest numbers.)* **Find the range.** *(15)* Write the range on the board.

Give Frequent Feedback ➤ Have small groups of students brainstorm ideas for remembering the meaning of each term. Students may observe, for example, that *median* and *middle* both have the same number of letters. *Mode* and *most* have the same number of letters and both words begin with the letter *m*. *Range* and *minus* also have the same number of letters.

Have each student write "mean," "median," "mode," and "range" on a separate card. Hold up a large card that says "most." **Show me the card with the word that has to do with "most."** Check that students show the "mode" card. **Yes, the mode tells which number is shown the most.** Continue the activity, using each term at least once. Then have each group come up with a list of numbers that they can use to find the mean, the median, the mode, and the range. Ask them to share their numbers with the class and explain how to find each measure for the data.

Circle Graphs

USE WITH LESSON 5-7

ACTIVATE PRIOR KNOWLEDGE/BUILD BACKGROUND; ACCESS CONTENT

Objective Complete circle graphs based on data given, and interpret given circle graphs.

Materials Circle Models (Teaching Tool 51)

Vocabulary Circle graph

ESL Strategies

Use before **LEARN**   ⏱ 10 MIN

Connect to Prior Knowledge of Math ➤ Display a <u>circle graph</u> like the one shown below. **Why do you think this graph is called a circle graph?** *(It is shaped like a circle.)* Remind students of the other types of graphs they have learned about. **A circle graph is another way to show information visually.**

Use Manipulatives ➤ Divide the class into groups of 3 students. Distribute 1 circle model to each group. **Suppose this circle is a pizza. Divide the pizza so that each of you gets an equal share.** When students have finished, ask: **How can you tell that you each have an equal share?** *(The 3 sections are the same size.)*

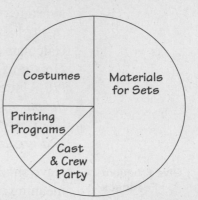

Provide more circle models and repeat the activity with different distributions. For example: **Divide the pizza so that (Student 1) has the biggest share and (Student 3) has the smallest share.**

Choosing an Appropriate Graph

USE WITH LESSON 5-8

ACTIVATE PRIOR KNOWLEDGE/BUILD BACKGROUND; ACCESS CONTENT

Objective Choose the most appropriate type of graph to represent a given set of data.

Vocabulary Bar graph, line graph, circle graph

ESL Strategies | *Use before* **LEARN**   ⏵ 10 MIN

Connect to Prior Knowledge of Math ➤ Tell students that they can use graphs to solve problems when the problem has a lot of data or when it helps to visualize the problem. **To use a graph to solve a problem, you need to know what kind of graph to make. When would you use a double <u>bar graph</u>?** *(When there is information about 2 groups)* **A <u>line graph</u>?** *(When data changes over time)* **A stem-and-leaf plot?** *(When the data are a list of many numbers)* **A <u>circle graph</u>?** *(To show parts of a whole)*

Use Small-Group Interactions ➤ Write the following examples on the board without their graph types. Read each example together with students. Have small groups of students match each example with one of the graph types. **Tell which kind of graph would best show this information. Explain why.** After students respond, write the correct graph type next to each example on the board.

    1. the test scores of 20 students *(Stem-and-leaf plot)*

    2. the number of boys and girls in each grade in a school *(Double bar graph)*

    3. how Janell spent her $10 allowance *(Circle graph)*

    4. the temperature every hour from 9 A.M. to 3 P.M. *(Line graph)*

Problem-Solving Skill: Writing to Compare

EXTEND LANGUAGE

Objective Interpret line and double bar graphs. Describe trends in data represented by line and double bar graphs.

ESL Strategies   *Use before* **LEARN**   ⏱ 5 MIN

Connect to Prior Experiences ➤ Have students think about baseball games they have either seen or participated in. Then ask volunteers to define the difference between a line drive and a pop fly. **What is the same about the two?** *(The batter gets a hit.)* **What is difference between the two?** *(In a line drive, the ball goes more or less directly from the bat to the field; In a pop fly, the ball goes high in the air and then comes down.)* **You have just compared two types of hits. You said what was the same about them and what was different. We can do the same thing with graphs of data.**

Use Pictures ➤ Draw two stick figures on the board, both at the same level and quite close to one another. Tell students that each figure represents the batter at home plate. Ask a volunteer to draw the trajectory of a line drive from one of the figures. Then ask another volunteer to draw the trajectory of a pop fly from the second figure. **You know that line graphs show change over time. Do each of these drawings show change over time?** *(Yes)* **How?** *(By showing the position of the baseball during the time it's in the air)* Draw a horizontal line beginning at the feet of the stick figures and extending across the board to the end of the drawn trajectories. Write 0 beneath the batters. **If this were the horizontal axis of a line graph, what interval could we use?** *(Sample answer: 1 second)* Then draw a vertical line beginning at the stick figures' feet and extending up to the top of the board. **If this were the vertical axis of a line graph, what interval could we use?** *(Sample answer: 5 feet)* Lead a discussion in which students use mathematical language to compare the graphs of the two types of hit.

Predicting Outcomes

EXTEND LANGUAGE

Objective Identify events and favorable outcomes, and determine if an outcome is equally likely, impossible, less likely, more likely, or certain.

Materials Paper bag; yellow, red, and blue colored cards; 6-sided number cube

Vocabulary Outcome

ESL Strategies   *Use before* **LEARN**   ⏱ 5–10 MIN

Have Students Report Back Orally ➤ Show students 1 yellow, 1 red, and 1 blue card as you put them in a paper bag. **I am going to take 1 card from the bag without looking. What are the possible colors?** *(Yellow, red, blue)* **We say that yellow, red, and blue**

are possible <u>outcomes</u>. Pick a card and show it to the class. **What is the outcome?** *(Students should name the color of the card.)* Pick out the other 2 cards, each time asking: **What is the outcome?**

Show the students a six-sided number cube. **How many outcomes are possible?** *(6)* Toss the number cube several times. **What are the possible outcomes on this number cube?** *(1, 2, 3, 4, 5, 6)*

What are some words you can use to compare numbers? *(Sample answers: Least, greatest, most, more, greater than, less than)* Add 2 more red cards and 4 more blue cards to the bag and repeat the demonstration. **Now there are 2 more red cards and 4 more blue cards. Do you expect me to pick a blue card or a yellow card?** *(Blue)* **Why?** *(There are 5 blue cards and only 1 yellow card in the bag.)* **We say that choosing blue is more likely than choosing yellow. What would we say about choosing yellow?** *(It is less likely than choosing blue.)* Have students use phrases like these as you continue to compare the likelihood of choosing different colors. Have them include the use of *least* and *most* when you explore different numbers of more than 2 colors.

Listing Outcomes

USE WITH LESSON 5-11

ACCESS CONTENT

Objective Find all possible outcomes of an event by making a tree diagram or by multiplying.

Materials *(per pair)* 1 coin; 3 connecting cubes (red, blue, and yellow)

Vocabulary Tree diagram

ESL Strategies *Use before* **LEARN**   ⏱ 15 MIN

Use Graphic Organizers ➤ Distribute the coins and cubes to each pair of students. Have them flip the coin several times. **How many possible outcomes are there with the coin?** *(2)* **What are they?** *(Heads, tails)* Draw a <u>tree diagram</u> on the board. Connect the word "coin" to the word "heads" with 1 line. Then connect "coin" to the word "tails" with another line. Now have them examine the connecting cubes. **How many possible outcomes are there?** *(3)* **What are they?** *(Red, yellow, blue)* Draw a separate tree diagram connecting the word "cube" to the words "red," "yellow," and "blue" with separate lines. **This is called a tree diagram.**

Why do you think so? *(It has branches, or parts, that connect the related information.)*

Coin Side	Cube Color	Possible Outcomes

Tree diagram:
- heads → red → heads, red
- heads → yellow → heads, yellow
- heads → blue → heads, blue
- tails → red → tails, red
- tails → yellow → tails, yellow
- tails → blue → tails, blue

Use Manipulatives ➤ Tell students to flip the coin then pick a connecting cube. Have them repeat several times. As they do, guide them in making a tree diagram like the one above where there are 3 color choices for each side of the coin. Explain that this diagram can help answer the question: **What are the possible outcomes for flipping a coin and choosing a cube?** Have students write each coin/cube combination in the last column of the tree diagram.

Expressing Probability as a Fraction

USE WITH LESSON 5-12

ACTIVATE PRIOR KNOWLEDGE/BUILD BACKGROUND; ACCESS CONTENT

Objective Use fractions to represent the probabilities of events, and use probability to decide if a game is fair or unfair.

Materials Connecting cubes (red, blue, yellow); number cards for 0–10

Vocabulary Probability

ESL Strategies **Use before** **LEARN** 🕐 15 MIN

Connect to Prior Knowledge of Language ➤ Write some sentences on the board using the word *probably,* such as: "It will probably rain tomorrow," and "I will probably go to the game this Friday."

Ask volunteers to use *probably* in their own sentences.

If something will probably happen, do we mean it is likely or not likely to happen? *(Likely)* **When we measure how likely something is, we measure its <u>probability</u>. What do I mean when I say there is a high probability that it will rain tomorrow?** *(It is likely to rain tomorrow.)* **What do I mean when I say there is a low probability that I will go to the game on Friday?** *(You are not likely to go.)*

Expand Student Responses ➤ Write the fractions $\frac{2}{10}$, $\frac{3}{10}$, and $\frac{5}{10}$ on the board. **Remember that these fractions can be read as "2 out of 10," "3 out of 10," and "5 out of 10."**

Have students repeat these phrases aloud. Display 3 yellow, 2 red, and 5 blue connecting cubes. **How many cubes do I have in all?** *(10)* **How many of the 10 cubes are yellow?** *(3 out of 10 are yellow.)* Encourage students to answer with the complete sentence. Circle $\frac{3}{10}$ on the board. Repeat the process for red and blue cubes.

We can show the probability of an outcome as a fraction. What is the probability that I will choose a blue cube? *(5 out of 10)* Continue with similar questions until students understand that a fraction is one way to show a probability.

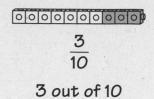

$$\frac{3}{10}$$

3 out of 10

Problem-Solving Applications: Population Growth

USE WITH LESSON 5-13

ACCESS CONTENT

Objective Review and apply key concepts, skills, and strategies learned in this and previous chapters.

ESL Strategies

Use before **LEARN**

🕐 10–15 MIN

Use Small-Group ➤ Assign students to small groups. Write the following data on the board and
Interactions   have students copy them.

State	1920	1990
Arizona	2.9	32.3
Colorado	9.1	31.8
Utah	5.5	21.0

Have students work together to plan making a graph of the data. Have them discuss the best type of graph to use. To prompt them, you might ask them questions such as, "What do the data show?" and "What type of graph shows a comparison of two pieces of data?" Then have groups work together to make a graph of the data. When they are finished, have each group exchange its graph with a neighboring group and have them explain the graph and how they made it, including choice of scale, color, and so on.

Geometric Ideas

ACCESS CONTENT; EXTEND LANGUAGE

Objective Identify important geometric terms relating to lines, parts of a line, angles, and planes.

Materials *(per pair)* Small bead; piece of uncooked spaghetti; sheet of paper; 3 index cards

Vocabulary Point, line segment, plane

ESL Strategies *Use before* CHECK ✓   ⏱ 10 MIN

Use Real Objects ➤ Write the following terms on the board: "<u>point</u>", "<u>line segment</u>", and "<u>plane</u>." Invite students to read the words together with you. Then group students into pairs and have each pair write each of the terms on a separate index card. Distribute a bead, a piece of spaghetti, and a sheet of paper to each pair. **You have learned the meaning of** *point, line segment,* **and** *plane.* **Match each vocabulary card you made with the object that best shows it.** *(Bead = point; spaghetti = line segment; paper = plane)*

Have Students Report Back Orally ➤ Ask each pair of students to choose one of their card/object pairs and present it to the class. **Why did you choose that object? How does it represent the word?**

Measuring and Classifying Angles

6-2

ACCESS CONTENT; ACTIVATE PRIOR KNOWLEDGE/BUILD BACKGROUND

Objective Measure and draw angles, and classify angles according to their measures.

Materials Ruler; *(per student)* flexible straw

Vocabulary Angle, vertex, degree

ESL Strategies *Use before* LEARN   ⏱ 10 MIN

Use Real Objects ➤ Give each student a flexible straw. **An <u>angle</u> is a shape that is made when 2 rays meet at the same point. You can bend this straw in different ways to show different angles.** Encourage students to bend the straw to make angles. **What do angles look like? What do all angles have in common?** Accept all reasonable answers, but guide students to understand that an angle has 2 sides and a bend, or <u>vertex</u>, where the sides meet.

Connect to Prior Knowledge of Math ➤ Show students the ruler and model measuring the length of an object in the room in inches. Ask a volunteer to read the measurement on the ruler.

(Sample answer: 3 in.) **An inch is a unit of measurement that describes length. What other units do we use to describe length?** *(Sample answers: feet, meters, miles)* **There are also other kinds of units, like the unit that measures the size of an angle. That unit is the <u>degree</u>.** Invite students to say the word *degree* after you. Draw the degree symbol (°) on the board. **This is the symbol that stands for degrees. In this lesson, you will learn about the size of angles and how to measure angles in degrees.**

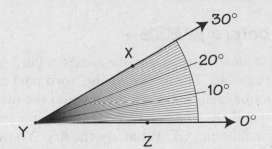

Segments and Angles Related to Circles

USE WITH LESSON 6-3

ACCESS CONTENT

Objective Identify relationships between parts of a circle such as center, radius, diameter, chord, and central angle.

Materials *(per student)* Compass; ruler

Vocabulary Center, radius, diameter, chord

ESL Strategies   **Use before** **CHECK** ✓   ⏱ 10–15 MIN

Use Manipulatives ➤
Give each student a sheet of paper, a pencil, a ruler, and a compass. Say and write the following directions one at a time on the board. Have students carry out the directions. Be sure to review the meaning of any words that students do not understand.

Draw a circle of any size that fits on the paper.

Draw and label the <u>center</u> of the circle A.

Draw and label the <u>diameter</u> $\overline{BC}$.

Draw and label a <u>radius</u> $\overline{AD}$.

Draw and label a <u>chord</u> $\overline{EF}$.

Use ➤ Peer Questioning
Ask students to take turns showing their completed drawings to a small group. Have the presenter ask questions such as, "Where is the chord?" or "Where is the radius?" Direct the other students in the group to answer the questions. Display the circles.

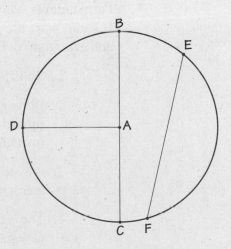

Polygons

Objective Identify and classify polygons.

Vocabulary Polygon, triangle, quadrilateral

ESL Strategies *Use before* LEARN   ⏱ 10 MIN

Focus on Form ➤ Direct students' attention to the names of the 5 <u>polygons</u> at the top of Student Book Page 340. **The prefix, or the word part at the beginning, of each of these names tells you something about the meaning of the word.** Make a two-column chart headed with "Prefix" in the left column and "Meaning" in the right column. Ask: **What are the first 3 letters of triangle?** Write "tri-" in the first row of the left column. Continue for the other prefixes.

Focus on Meaning ➤ Point to "tri-" in the chart. **A <u>triangle</u> has 3 sides. What do you think the prefix *tri-* means?** *(3)* Point to "quad-" in the chart. **A <u>quadrilateral</u> has 4 sides. What do you think the prefix *quad-* means?** *(4)* Complete the chart for *pent-, hex-,* and *oct-*. **The prefix *hept-* means 7. What is a heptagon?** *(A polygon with 7 sides)* Display the chart as a reference.

Classifying Triangles

Objective Identify and classify triangles.

Materials *(per pair)* 16 index cards

Vocabulary Right triangle, obtuse triangle, acute triangle

ESL Strategies *Use before* CHECK ✓   ⏱ 15 MIN

Use Small-Group ➤ Remind students that they know the names and definitions of different kinds
Interactions of triangles. **We are going to play a game to practice triangle vocabulary.** Have each pair of students make 16 game cards—8 cards with the terms in the table below and 8 cards with the students' own definitions for each term. Pair students who are learning English with students who are fluent speakers. If some pairs are struggling with any terms, use examples to help them recall and articulate definitions. Post and review the rules of the game.

1. Shuffle the cards and place them facedown in a 4-by-4 array.

2. Player 1 turns over any 2 cards. If a term and its definition are turned over, the player keeps the cards. If not, the cards are turned facedown in the same positions.

3. Player 2 takes a turn. Players alternate turns until all of the cards are matched.

4. The game can be repeated by shuffling the cards and starting a new game.

Term	Definition
triangle	a polygon with three sides and three angles
acute triangle	a triangle with three acute angles
right triangle	a triangle with one right angle
obtuse triangle	a triangle with one obtuse angle
equilateral triangle	a triangle with three equal-length sides
isosceles triangle	a triangle with at least two equal-length sides
scalene triangle	a triangle with no sides of equal length
protractor	a tool used for measuring and drawing angles

Classifying Quadrilaterals

USE WITH LESSON
6-6

ACCESS CONTENT

Objective Identify and classify quadrilaterals.

Vocabulary Parallelogram, trapezoid, rectangle, rhombus, square

ESL Strategies | ***Use before*** CHECK ✓ | ⏱ 10 MIN

Use Demonstration ➤ Write and say an example of a riddle. Example: **I am a polygon with 3 sides. What am I?** *(Triangle)* Explain that these types of riddles describe a figure and what makes it different from other figures. It ends with the question, "What am I?"

Use Small-Group Interactions ➤ Divide the class into 5 groups. Assign each group one of the quadrilaterals— parallelogram, trapezoid, rectangle, rhombus, or square—and have them work together to write a riddle. When the groups are finished, have each one take a turn reading its riddle to the class. Ask the other groups: **What is the answer to the riddle?**

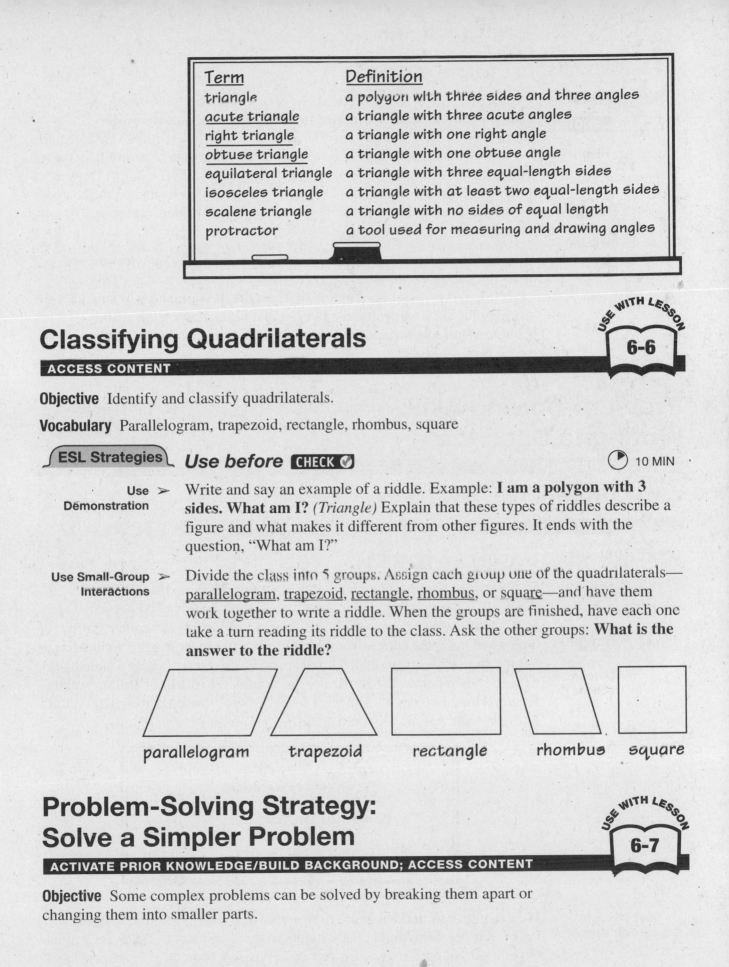

parallelogram   trapezoid   rectangle   rhombus   square

Problem-Solving Strategy: Solve a Simpler Problem

USE WITH LESSON
6-7

ACTIVATE PRIOR KNOWLEDGE/BUILD BACKGROUND; ACCESS CONTENT

Objective Some complex problems can be solved by breaking them apart or changing them into smaller parts.

Use before **LEARN** 🕐 10 MIN

Connect to Prior ➤ Write $5\frac{5}{8} + 4\frac{1}{12} + 8\frac{3}{5}$ vertically on the board. Write $6 + 4$ vertically next to it.
Experiences **Which problem would be easier to solve? Why?** *(Sample answer: The problem on the right; it has only 2 numbers and no fractions.)* Draw a triangle on the board and a 12-sided figure to the right. **Which figure would be easier to trace? Why?** *(Sample answer: The triangle; it has fewer sides.)* Draw a 10-inch straight line and a 2-foot squiggly line next to each other on the board. **Which figure would be easier to measure? Why?** *(Sample answer: The straight line; it is shorter and straighter.)*

Paraphrase Ideas ➤ **Why are some problems easier to solve than others?** *(Sample answers: Some have smaller numbers; some have numbers that are easier to work with; you can solve some with one step.)* **In this lesson, you will learn a new strategy for solving problems. If a problem has many steps or has numbers that are difficult to work with, you might solve a simpler or an easier problem first.**

Problem-Solving Skill: Writing to Describe

EXTEND LANGUAGE

USE WITH LESSON **6-8**

Objective Describe similarities and differences in geometric figures.

Materials *(per pair)* Index cards

ESL Strategies

Use before **CHECK** 🕐 5 MIN

Focus on Form ➤ **In this lesson, you are learning about how to describe things.** Write "English: describe" and "Latin: de + scribere" on the board. **Many words in English and other languages come from an old language called Latin. The word *describe* comes from the Latin words meaning "to write."** Point out the similarities between the English and Latin terms. Present a table like the one shown below. **Do you know the Spanish, French, or Italian words for *describe*?** Use any student answers to help you complete the chart. **What does *describe* mean?** *(To write about something or explain it in words)*

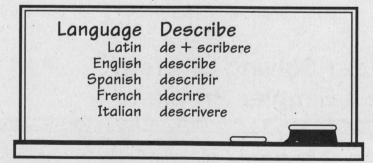

Language	Describe
Latin	de + scribere
English	describe
Spanish	describir
French	decrire
Italian	descrivere

Have Students ➤ **We are going to make a game to practice describing geometric figures.**
Create Test Items Pass out index cards and guide students working in pairs to make flash cards. On one side of each index card, have pairs draw a geometric figure and label

it. On the other side, have them write a description of the figure without naming it. Have pairs exchange cards. Partners can quiz each other by alternately showing the side with the geometric figure and asking for a description and showing the side with the description and asking for the name of the figure. After they have exchanged cards, give pairs an opportunity to provide one another feedback about words and phrases that could be included in their descriptions.

Congruence and Similarity

USE WITH LESSON 6-9

EXTEND LANGUAGE

Objective Identify congruent figures and similar figures.

Materials Paper; tracing paper; markers

Vocabulary Congruent figures, similar figures

ESL Strategies *Use before* **LEARN** 🕐 5 MIN

Focus on Meaning ➤ Have students work in pairs. Direct one student to draw a simple shape on the paper and the other to trace it by laying down tracing paper. **Put the drawings side by side. What do you notice about the shapes of the 2 figures? What about the sizes?** *(The figures have the same shape and size.)* **Figures with the same shape and size are called** <u>congruent figures</u>. Write "congruent" on the board. Practice pronouncing the word with students.

Direct one student to draw a simple figure on a new sheet of paper. Have the other partner lay tracing paper over it and draw the same figure about 1 in. *inside* the original. You may want to model how to make this kind of tracing for the students first. **Put the drawings side by side. What do you notice about the shapes of the figures? What about the sizes?** *(The figures have the same shape but a different size.)* **Figures with the same shape but different sizes are** <u>similar figures</u>. Write "similar" on the board. Practice pronouncing the term with students.

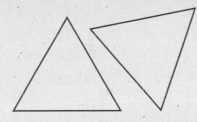

congruent

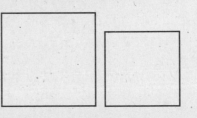

similar

Transformations

ACCESS CONTENT

Objective Determine whether a pair of congruent figures are related by a slide (translation), flip (reflection), or turn (rotation).

Materials Power Polygon Template (Teaching Tool 26)

Vocabulary Slide (translation), flip (reflection), turn (rotation)

ESL Strategies *Use before* **LEARN**   ⏱ 5 MIN

Use Demonstration ➤ Use an overhead projector with a rectangle shape or a large paper rectangle on the board to demonstrate slides, flips, and turns. Put the figure in a start position, then slide the figure along a straight path to a new location. Say: **This is a <u>slide</u>, or <u>translation</u>.** Draw a straight line on the board or on an overhead transparency, and model how to flip the figure over the line. Say: **This is a <u>flip</u>, or <u>reflection</u>.** Put your finger on a corner of the figure and rotate it around that point. Say: **This is a <u>turn</u>, or <u>rotation</u>.** Repeat these exercises a few more times. As you perform each, have students answer aloud whether you are showing a translation, reflection, or rotation.

Give Frequent Feedback ➤ Distribute a triangle to each student. **Slide the triangle.** Observe students' actions and give feedback by modeling the answer with a large paper triangle. Make comments such as: **That's right. You slide the triangle by moving it in a straight line.** Repeat for a flip and a turn. Continue to provide feedback after each transformation.

 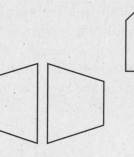 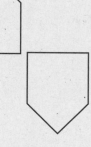

slide   flip   turn

Symmetry

ACCESS CONTENT

Objective Identify and make symmetrical figures and draw a line or lines of symmetry.

Materials *(per student)* Construction paper square

Vocabulary Symmetric, line of symmetry

Use before LEARN

Use Manipulatives ➤ Give each student a construction paper square. **Fold this square in half.** When students finish folding the paper, say: **You folded the square so that the 2 parts match exactly. We say that the 2 sides are symmetric.** Write "symmetric" on the board and help students with the pronunciation.

Use Small-Group ➤ **What separates the 2 symmetric parts of your square?** *(The fold, a line)*
Interactions **This is called a line of symmetry. There are 3 more ways to fold the square to show symmetry.** Have students consult in small groups to find the 3 ways by folding and refolding the square. **How many lines are on your square?** *(4)* **You found 4 lines of symmetry.** Write "lines of symmetry" on the board and help students with the pronunciation.

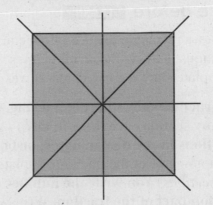

Problem-Solving Applications:
Skyscrapers

USE WITH LESSON
6-12

ACCESS CONTENT

Objective Review and apply key concepts, skills, and strategies learned in this and previous chapters.

Materials *(per pair)* Power polygons for circle, square, triangle, rectangle; graph paper; ruler; 4 index cards with terms "line of symmetry," "flip," "slide," and "turn," one on each card

Use before LEARN

Use Manipulatives ➤ Have one partner choose a Polygon, identify it by name, and trace it onto graph paper. Have the other partner select a card. **Read the word or words and explain what they mean.** *(Sample answer: line of symmetry; a line of symmetry is a line that divides a figure into two identical halves)* The first partner then flips, slides, or turns the power polygon to follow the direction on the card or uses the ruler to draw a line of symmetry through the figure on the paper. Partners alternate roles, repeating the activity with each of the index cards. They then repeat the activity for each of the polygons.

Meanings of Fractions

ACCESS CONTENT

USE WITH LESSON
7-1

Objective Identify and show fractional parts of regions and sets and locations on a number line.

Materials *(per student)* Crayons

Vocabulary Fraction, numerator, denominator

ESL Strategies   *Use before* **LEARN**   ⏱ 10 MIN

Use ➤
Demonstration
Draw a rectangle divided into 4 equal sections on the board. Shade 3 of the sections, leaving the dividing lines visible in the figure. Draw a <u>fraction</u> template showing two empty boxes separated by a fraction bar.

A fraction shows part of a whole, or group. Look at this rectangle. How many sections are there in all? *(4 sections)* **You write the total number of sections in the <u>denominator</u>, or bottom part of the fraction.** Write 4 in the denominator of the fraction template. **How many sections are shaded?** *(3 sections)* **You write the number of shaded sections in the <u>numerator</u>, or top part of the fraction.** Write 3 in the numerator. Point to each part of the fraction and say, $\frac{3}{4}$ **of this rectangle is shaded.**

Use Small-Group ➤
Interactions
Have students fold a piece of paper into fourths, then unfold it. Direct each student to shade some number of sections, then trade his or her paper with a partner. **Look at your partner's rectangle. How many sections are there in all?** *(4 sections)* **How many sections are shaded?** *(Answers will vary.)* **What fraction of the rectangle is shaded?** *(Answers will vary.)* Have students write the fraction.

Fractions and Division

ACTIVATE PRIOR KNOWLEDGE/BUILD BACKGROUND; ACCESS CONTENT

USE WITH LESSON
7-2

Objective Division can be used to divide objects into equal parts where the parts are fractions of a whole.

Materials *(per group)* 2 large paper circles; scissors

ESL Strategies   *Use before* **LEARN**   ⏱ 10 MIN

Use ➤
Brainstorming
Divide the class into groups of 3 students. **Suppose that each circle is an apple pie. You have 2 pies to share equally among the 3 of you. How much pie will each of you get?** Give students an opportunity to discuss possible strategies for solving the problem.

If you have only 1 apple pie, how would you divide it so that each of you gets an equal piece? *(Divide it into thirds.)* **Cut apart each of your pies into 3 equal pieces. How many pieces do you have in all?** *(6 pieces)* **Now pass out the pieces so each of you gets the same amount of pie. How many pieces did each of you get?** *(2 pieces)* **If one pie can be divided into 3 pieces, what fraction of a pie did each of you get?** $(\frac{2}{3})$ **Write "2 pies ÷ 3 people," 2 ÷ 3, and $\frac{2}{3}$ on the board. Help students relate the expressions.**

$$2 \text{ pies} \div 3 \text{ people} \qquad 2 \div 3 \qquad \frac{2}{3}$$

Mixed Numbers

USE WITH LESSON **7-3**

ACCESS CONTENT; EXTEND LANGUAGE

Objective Express fractions greater than 1 as mixed numbers or improper fractions.

Materials *(per group)* Pennies; nickels; red and yellow cubes; large and small paper clips

Vocabulary Mixed number

ESL Strategies | *Use before* **LEARN** | ⏱ 5 MIN

Use Real Objects ➤ Place the objects in the center of a table for each group of students. Have students make a pile with pennies and nickels. **How many different kinds of coins do you see?** *(2)* **We have mixed different coins.** Have them make a pile with red and yellow cubes. **How many different colors do you see?** *(2)* **We have mixed different colors.** Have them make a pile with large and small paper clips. **How many different sizes do you see?** *(2)* **We have mixed different sizes.**

Focus on Meaning ➤ Write five <u>mixed numbers</u> on the board. **These numbers are called *mixed numbers*. Why do you think so?** *(They mix different kinds of numbers.)* **What two kinds of numbers are in a mixed number?** *(A whole number and a fraction)*

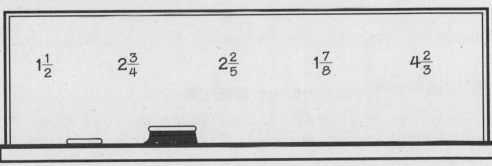

$$1\frac{1}{2} \qquad 2\frac{3}{4} \qquad 2\frac{2}{5} \qquad 1\frac{7}{8} \qquad 4\frac{2}{3}$$

Estimating Fractional Amounts

ACCESS CONTENT

Objective Estimate fractional parts of regions.

Materials *(per student)* Paper square; rectangle strip; paper circle; crayons

Vocabulary Benchmark fractions

ESL Strategies *Use before* **LEARN**   ⏱ 15 MIN

Use Demonstration ➤ A <u>benchmark fraction</u> is a fraction you can use to estimate amounts or measurements. Benchmark fractions include $\frac{1}{2}$, $\frac{1}{3}$, and $\frac{1}{4}$. Write $\frac{1}{2}$, $\frac{1}{3}$, and $\frac{1}{4}$ on the board. Draw a square on the board, and divide it into four equal parts. Shade one fourth plus a small portion of a second fourth. **What would you estimate the shaded part to be?** ($\frac{1}{4}$) Draw a circle on the board and divide it in half. Shade a little less than half of the circle. **What would you estimate the shaded part to be?** ($\frac{1}{2}$) Repeat the example with a rectangle that is shaded about $\frac{2}{3}$. Continue the process with other shapes and other benchmark fractions if necessary.

Use Manipulatives ➤ **Fractions can be shown in different shapes and sizes. Let us make three models of $\frac{1}{4}$.** Have students fold a paper square into four equal sections. Students should shade one section. Have them repeat the activity for the rectangle and circle. **Which benchmark fraction does each of the models show?** ($\frac{1}{4}$) Encourage students to use the models as a reference when solving the exercises in lesson 7-4.

Fractions and Mixed Numbers on the Number Line

ACTIVATE PRIOR KNOWLEDGE/BUILD BACKGROUND; ACCESS CONTENT

Objective Identify and locate fractions and mixed numbers on a number line.

Materials Index cards, each labeled with one of the following: 0, $\frac{1}{2}$, 1, $1\frac{1}{3}$, $2\frac{1}{4}$, and 3

ESL Strategies *Use before* **LEARN**   ⏱ 15 MIN

Connect to Prior Knowledge of Math ➤ Draw a large number line from 0 to 3 on the board. **What does a number line show?** (*The order of numbers from least to greatest*) **In which direction**

do you read a number line? *(From left to right)* **Where are the smallest numbers?** *(On the left)* **The greatest numbers?** *(On the right)*

Use Total Physical Response ➤ Have 6 volunteers come up to the front of the room. Give each one an index card to hold up for the class to see. **We want to find out where each of these numbers belongs on the number line. Which number belongs on the left?** *(Zero)* Have the class discuss and tell the student holding the card with the number 0 where to stand under the number line on the board. Repeat for each of the other fraction cards until the number line is complete.

Problem-Solving Skill: Extra or Missing Information

USE WITH LESSON 7-6

ACCESS CONTENT; EXTEND LANGUAGE

Objective Solve problems involving too much information by using only the information needed, and decide when there is not enough information to solve a problem.

Materials *(per student)* Crayons or markers

ESL Strategies   *Use before* **LEARN**   ⏱ 10 MIN

Focus on Meaning ➤ Have each student draw a basket with 5 apples, 3 bananas, and 2 oranges. Write the following problems on the board.

> How many more apples than oranges are there?
> How much do the apples cost in all?

Read the first question aloud and have students discuss which information they need from the picture to solve the problem. **Is there any information in the picture that you do not need?** *(Yes)* **What is it?**

(The number of bananas) Explain that sometimes you have more information than you need to solve a problem. **How would you solve the problem?** *(Subtract 2 from 5; 5 − 2 = 3 apples)* Read the second problem aloud. **Can you solve this problem?** *(No)* **Why or why not?** *(I do not know how much 1 apple costs.)* Explain that sometimes there is not enough information to solve a problem. **What else do you need to know to solve the problem?** *(The cost of 1 apple)*

Understanding Equivalent Fractions

USE WITH LESSON 7-7

ACCESS CONTENT

Objective Identify and write equivalent fractions.

Materials *(per student)* Fraction Strips (Teaching Tool 27)

Vocabulary Equivalent fractions

ESL Strategies

Paraphrase Ideas➤

Use before **LEARN**

⏱ 10 MIN

Divide the class into groups. Give each student $\frac{1}{2}$ strips, $\frac{1}{4}$ strips, and $\frac{1}{6}$ strips. **Make one half in three ways: using only $\frac{1}{2}$ strips, using only $\frac{1}{4}$ strips, and using only $\frac{1}{6}$ strips.** Observe students as they work together.

When students finish, ask, **What do you notice about the 3 strips that you put together?** *(They are the same length.)* **When fraction strips are the same length, they show the same fraction. In this case, each of your strips shows the fraction $\frac{1}{2}$. How many $\frac{1}{2}$ strips did you use to show one half?** *(1)* Write $1 \times \frac{1}{2} = \frac{1}{2}$ on the board. **How many $\frac{1}{4}$ strips did you use to show one half?** *(2)* Write $2 \times \frac{1}{4} = \frac{2}{4}$ on the board. **How many $\frac{1}{6}$ strips did you use to show one half?** *(3)* Write $3 \times \frac{1}{6} = \frac{3}{6}$ on the board. **Equivalent fractions name the same fraction in different ways. You found three different ways to write the same fraction.** Write $\frac{1}{2} = \frac{2}{4} = \frac{3}{6}$ on the board.

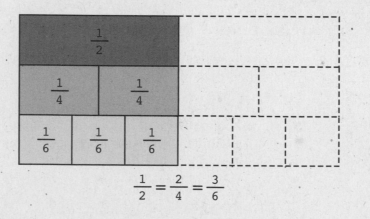

$$\frac{1}{2} = \frac{2}{4} = \frac{3}{6}$$

Equivalent Fractions

ACCESS CONTENT

Objective Identify fractions that are equivalent and find fractions equivalent to a given fraction using models and/or a computational procedure.

Materials *(per pair)* Index cards, each labeled with one of the following: $\frac{1}{2}$, $\frac{1}{3}$, $\frac{1}{4}$, $\frac{2}{3}$, and $\frac{3}{4}$; number cube labeled 1 through 6

Vocabulary Equivalent fractions

ESL Strategies   *Use before* **CHECK** ✓   🕐 5 MIN

Use Small-Group Interactions ➤ Arrange students into pairs. Have each pair shuffle and place the fraction cards facedown in a stack. Have one partner draw the top card and have the other partner toss the number cube. Then have partners work together to find an <u>equivalent fraction</u> by multiplying the numerator and denominator of the fraction by the number on the number cube. **What is the equivalent fraction?** *(Answers will vary.)* Have partners switch roles and repeat the activity for each fraction card.

Greatest Common Factor

ACTIVATE PRIOR KNOWLEDGE/BUILD BACKGROUND; ACCESS CONTENT

Objective Determine common factors and the greatest common factor of numbers.

Materials 2 identical objects

Vocabulary Greatest common factor

ESL Strategies   *Use before* **LEARN**   🕐 5 MIN

Connect to Prior Knowledge of Math ➤ **What does the word** *greatest* **mean?** *(Sample answers: The best, the most, the largest)* Write "greatest" on the board. Have students write sentences using the word *greatest*. Show students two identical objects, such as balls. **How are these balls alike?** *(They have the same color and shape.)* **In other words, the balls have a common color and a common shape.** Write "common" on the board.

Use Demonstration ➤ Write "factor" on the board and review its meaning with students. Write the numbers 20 and 30 on the board. **What are the factors of 20?** *(1, 2, 4, 5,*

10, 20) List each factor on the board as students answer. **What are the factors of 30?** *(1, 2, 3, 5, 6, 10, 15, 30)* List the factors of 30 on the board below the factors of 20.

What do I mean if I say two numbers have a *common* **factor?** *(Both numbers have the same factor.)* Direct students' attention to the lists on the board. **Which factors are common to both 20 and 30?** *(1, 2, 5, 10)* Underline each common factor as students answer. **What do you think the <u>greatest common factor</u> of two numbers is?** *(The largest number that is a factor of both numbers)* **What is the greatest common factor of 20 and 30?** *(10)* Circle the GCF.

Fractions in Simplest Form

USE WITH LESSON 7-10

ACTIVATE PRIOR KNOWLEDGE/BUILD BACKGROUND; ACCESS CONTENT

Objective Identify fractions that are in simplest form and find the simplest form of a fraction.

Materials *(per student)* Index card

Vocabulary Simplest form

ESL Strategies

Connect to Prior Knowledge of Math

Use before **CHECK ✓**

⏲ 10 MIN

Write $\frac{2}{3}$ on the board. **What is the numerator?** *(2)* **What is the denominator?** *(3)* **Is there a number other than 1 that you can divide into both 2 and 3?** *(No)* **If only the number 1 divides into both the numerator and denominator, the fraction is in <u>simplest form</u>.**

Write $\frac{5}{10}$ on the board. **What is the numerator?** *(5)* **What is the denominator?** *(10)* **Is the fraction $\frac{5}{10}$ in simplest form?** *(No)* **Why?** *(The number 5 divides into both 5 and 10.)* **Let us divide both the numerator and denominator by 5. What fraction do we get?** *($\frac{1}{2}$)* Cross out 5 and 10 and replace the numerator and denominator with 1 and 2. **Is there a number other than 1 that you can divide into both 1 and 2?** *(No)* **In what form is $\frac{1}{2}$?** *(Simplest form)*

This fraction is not in the simplest form because I can divide the numerator and denominator by 3.

Understanding Comparing Fractions

USE WITH LESSON **7-11**

ACCESS CONTENT

Objective Determine which of two fractions is greater or less and write a comparison.

Materials *(per pair)* Fraction Strips (Teaching Tool 27)

 **ESL Strategies**   *Use before* **LEARN**   🕐 5 MIN

Use Manipulatives ➤ Divide the class into pairs. Write $\frac{2}{3}$ ___ $\frac{1}{3}$ on the board. Have each partner model one of the fractions using fraction strips, then lay the models next to each other. **Look at which fraction strip is longer. Now tell me which fraction is greater.** ($\frac{2}{3}$) Complete the comparison on the board by writing a greater than symbol (>) in the blank. Have students read the inequality aloud with you: $\frac{2}{3}$ **is greater than** $\frac{1}{3}$.

Write $\frac{3}{8}$ ___ $\frac{3}{5}$ on the board. Have partners model and compare the fraction strips. **Which of these fractions is greater?** ($\frac{3}{5}$) Complete the comparison by writing a less than symbol (<) on the board. Have students read the inequality aloud with you: $\frac{3}{8}$ **is less than** $\frac{3}{5}$.

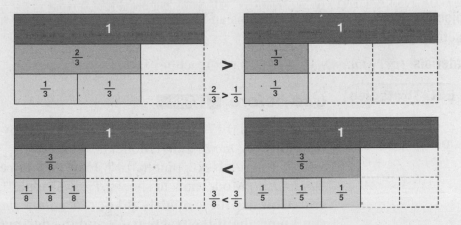

Comparing and Ordering Fractions and Mixed Numbers

USE WITH LESSON **7-12**

ACCESS CONTENT

Objective Compare and order fractions and mixed numbers.

Materials *(per group)* Fraction Strips (Teaching Tool 27)

Use before CHECK ✓   ◔ 10–15 MIN

Use Manipulatives ➤ Divide the class into groups. Write $\frac{3}{4}$, $1\frac{1}{4}$, $\frac{1}{4}$, $\frac{4}{4}$, and $\frac{2}{4}$ on the board. **What do these fractions have in common?** *(They have the same denominator.)* **How are they different?** *(They have different numerators; one is a mixed number.)* Have each group of students model the fractions using fraction strips. **Which fraction is the least?** $(\frac{1}{4})$ **How do you know?** *(It is the shortest strip.)* Repeat this line of questioning until students can name the 4 fractions in order from least to greatest. $(\frac{1}{4}, \frac{2}{4}, \frac{3}{4}, \frac{4}{4}, 1\frac{1}{4})$ Remind students that they can convert the mixed number into an improper fraction in order to compare it. Write them in order on the board. **When the denominators are the same, how do you put the fractions in order?** *(Look at the numerators and put them in order.)*

Repeat the activity for the fractions $\frac{1}{4}$, $\frac{1}{2}$, $\frac{1}{3}$, and $\frac{1}{6}$. **What do these fractions have in common?** *(They have the same numerator.)* **How are they different?** *(They have different denominators.)* Have each group of students model the fractions using fraction strips. **Which fraction is the least?** $(\frac{1}{6})$ **How do you know?** *(It is the shortest strip.)* Repeat this line of questioning until students can name the 4 fractions in order from least to greatest. $(\frac{1}{6}, \frac{1}{4}, \frac{1}{3}, \frac{1}{2})$ Write them in order on the board. **When the numerators are the same, how do you put the fractions in order?** *(The greater the denominator, the less the fraction's value.)*

Fractions and Decimals

ACCESS CONTENT

USE WITH LESSON
7-13

Objective Represent decimals (tenths and hundredths) as fractions and simple fractions as decimals.

Materials *(per student)* 10 × 10 Chart (Teaching Tool 3)

Use before LEARN   ◔ 10 MIN

Use ➤ Write $\frac{17}{100}$ and 0.17 on the board. Point to $\frac{17}{100}$. **How do you read this**
Demonstration **fraction?** *(17 hundredths)* Model how to show $\frac{17}{100}$ by shading 17 squares on a 10 × 10 grid. Next point to 0.17. **How do you read this decimal?** *(17 hundredths)* Model how to show 0.17 by shading 17 squares on a 10 × 10 grid. **How are these models alike?** *(They show the same thing.)* **So what do you know about the fraction $\frac{17}{100}$ and the decimal 0.17?** *(They are the same, or equal.)* Write $\frac{17}{100} = 0.17$ on the board. **You can write fractions as decimals and decimals as fractions.**

Use Small-Group ➤ Have students work in pairs. Have one partner model $\frac{35}{100}$ and the other model
Interactions 0.35. Then have students say the number that they modeled, compare their models, and discuss what they represent. Repeat with other equivalent fractions and decimals in hundredths.

$$\frac{17}{100} = 0.17$$

$$\frac{17}{100}$$

$$0.17$$

Fractions and Decimals on the Number Line

USE WITH LESSON 7-14

ACCESS CONTENT

Objective Label a point on a number line using a fraction and a decimal, and write a fraction and decimal for a point on a number line.

ESL Strategies | *Use before* **LEARN** | ⏱ 10 MIN

Use Small-Group Interactions ➤ Write the fractions $\frac{15}{100}$, $\frac{3}{10}$, and $\frac{41}{100}$ on the board. Have small groups of students work together to change the fractions to decimals. *(0.15, 0.30, 0.41)* Then write the decimals 0.25, 0.4, and 0.53 on the board and have the groups change the decimals to fractions. *($\frac{25}{100}$, $\frac{4}{10}$, $\frac{53}{100}$)* **Is it easier to change the fractions to decimals or the decimals to fractions?** *(Answers will vary.)* **Why?** *(Accept responses students can justify.)* Have students explain the processes that they used.

Use Graphic Organizers ➤ Write the numbers 0.8, $1\frac{1}{2}$, $\frac{3}{4}$, 2.25, 0.5 on the board. Draw a number line on the board. **How can you order fractions and decimals on a number line?** *(By making all of the numbers fractions or all of the numbers decimals.)* Have groups choose one method to use to order the numbers. Have volunteers fill in the number line on the board. Instruct them to write decimal numbers above the number line and fractions below the number line. *(0.5, 0.75, 0.8, 1.5, 2.25; $\frac{1}{2}$, $\frac{3}{4}$, $\frac{8}{10}$, $1\frac{1}{2}$, $2\frac{1}{4}$)*

Problem-Solving Strategy: Use Logical Reasoning

USE WITH LESSON 7-15

ACTIVATE PRIOR KNOWLEDGE/BUILD BACKGROUND; ACCESS CONTENT

Objective Use the information given in the problem to make conclusions.

ESL Strategies | *Use before* **LEARN** | ⏱ 10 MIN

Use Simulation ➤ Have 4 students line up at the front of the class. **Let us describe the order of these students by writing sentences about their places in line.** Write a descriptive statement on the board such as, "(Student 1) is in front of (Student 2)." Have students suggest similar sentences as you write them on the board. Elicit suggestions until there is enough information to describe the entire line.

Use Total ➤ Have the 4 students move to the side. **Let us use the information on the**
Physical Response **board to put the students back in order.** Ask volunteers to direct the
4 students how to stand using the directions on the board. When the students are in order, ask the class, **How did you make the line again?** *(I used the information on the board to solve the problem step-by-step.)*

Problem-Solving Applications: Extreme Machines

USE WITH LESSON
7-16

ACCESS CONTENT; EXTEND LANGUAGE

Objective Review and apply key concepts, skills, and strategies learned in this and previous chapters.

ESL Strategies | *Use before* **CHECK** ✓ | ⏵ 10 MIN

Use Small-Group ➤ Divide students into 3 groups. Write $\frac{2}{4}$ on the board and have a volunteer say
Interactions and explain its meaning. Assign one group to find the fraction in simplest form, another group to find an equivalent fraction, and the third group to find the decimal equivalent.

Have Students ➤ Have each group present the answer and explain its solution to the class.
Report Back *(Simplest form: divide numerator and denominator by the GCF (2) to get the*
Orally *simplest form of $\frac{1}{2}$; Equivalent fraction: multiply or divide numerator and denominator by the same number such as 3, possible answer is $\frac{6}{12}$; Decimal equivalent: Write an equivalent fraction with a denominator of 100 ($\frac{50}{100}$) and then write as a decimal, 0.5)*

Then write the fraction $\frac{6}{10}$ *(Simplest: $\frac{3}{5}$; equivalent possible answer: $\frac{12}{20}$; decimal: 0.6)* and repeat the activity, assigning a different role to each group. Repeat for $\frac{16}{20}$ *(Simplest: $\frac{4}{5}$; equivalent possible answer: $\frac{8}{10}$; decimal: 0.8),* assigning the third role to each group.

Adding and Subtracting Fractions with Like Denominators

USE WITH LESSON 8-1

ACTIVATE PRIOR KNOWLEDGE/BUILD BACKGROUND; ACCESS CONTENT

Objective Add or subtract fractions with like denominators.

Materials *(per pair)* 8 index cards

Vocabulary Like denominator

ESL Strategies　*Use before*　**LEARN**　　🕐 5–10 MIN

Connect to Prior Knowledge of Math ➤ Hold up two red balls, pieces of chalk, or other identical objects. **How are these objects alike?** *(Sample answer: They have the same shape and color.)* **What does it mean if objects are like or alike?** *(They are the same.)* Write $\frac{1}{2}$, $\frac{2}{3}$, $\frac{3}{4}$, and $\frac{5}{8}$ on the board. **What kinds of numbers are these?** *(Fractions)* **Which number in a fraction is the denominator?** *(The number on the bottom.)* Have students identify the denominator in each fraction. **What does it mean for two fractions to have <u>like denominators</u>?** *(They have the same denominator.)*

Use Small-Group Interactions ➤ Have each pair of students copy the following fractions onto index cards, one fraction per card: $\frac{1}{3}$, $\frac{2}{3}$, $\frac{1}{4}$, $\frac{3}{4}$, $\frac{3}{6}$, $\frac{5}{6}$, $\frac{3}{8}$, and $\frac{7}{8}$. **Shuffle the cards and spread them face–up on a desk.** Have one partner select a card and the other partner choose the fraction with a like denominator. Partners should discuss how they know the fractions have like denominators. Partners repeat the activity, alternating roles, until all of the cards are matched. Explain to students that they will use this skill when they add and subtract fractions.

Understanding Adding and Subtracting with Unlike Denominators

USE WITH LESSON 8-2

ACCESS CONTENT

Objective Find a common denominator for two fractions using fraction strips.

Materials *(per student)* Fraction Strips (Teaching Tool 27)

Vocabulary Common denominator

ESL Strategies   *Use before* **LEARN**   ⏱ 10 MIN

Use Manipulatives ➤ Write $\frac{1}{4}$ on the board and have students model $\frac{1}{4}$ using fourths fraction strips. **Now model the same fraction using eighths and twelfths.** ($\frac{2}{8}$; $\frac{3}{12}$) **Repeat the activity for $\frac{1}{3}$ using sixths and twelfths.** Have students place the $\frac{1}{4}$ models on the left and the $\frac{1}{3}$ models on the right. **Which kind of fraction strips did you use for both models?** *(twelfths)* **If you wanted to show $\frac{1}{4}$ and $\frac{1}{3}$ using the same kind of fractions strips, which could you use? Explain.** *(Twelfths because both fractions can be shown using twelfths.)* Explain that 12 is a <u>common denominator</u> for the fractions because you can use twelfth strips to model both.

Repeat the activity for $\frac{1}{2}$ as fourths and sixths and $\frac{1}{3}$ as sixths. **What is the common denominator? How do you know?** *(6; I can use the sixths strips to model $\frac{1}{2}$ and $\frac{1}{3}$.)* Repeat for $\frac{1}{2}$ and $\frac{1}{5}$.

Common Denominator: 12

Least Common Denominators

USE WITH LESSON 8-3

EXTEND LANGUAGE

Objective Find a common denominator for two fractions.

Materials Fraction Strips (Teaching Tool 27)

ESL Strategies   *Use before* **LEARN**   ⏱ 10 MIN

Connect to Prior ➤ Write $\frac{1}{6}$ and $\frac{5}{6}$ on the board. **Do these fractions have a common**
Knowledge of   **denominator? Explain.** *(Yes; both fractions have a 6 in the denominator)*
Math

Write $\frac{3}{4}$ and $\frac{1}{3}$ on the board. **Do these fractions have a common denominator? Explain.** *(No; the fractions have different numbers, 4 and 3, in the denominator.)* **One way to find a common denominator for two fractions is to multiply the denominators. What two numbers should I multiply to find a common denominator for $\frac{3}{4}$ and $\frac{1}{3}$?** *(4 in $\frac{3}{4}$ and 3 in $\frac{1}{3}$)* Circle the denominators in each fraction. **What is the common denominator?** *(12)* Ask students to discuss how they would write equivalent fractions for $\frac{3}{4}$ and $\frac{1}{3}$ using 12 as a denominator.

Have Students ➤ Assign each pair or small group of students two fractions with unlike
Report Back denominators, such as $\frac{2}{3}$ and $\frac{1}{2}$. Have them find the common denominator,
Orally then rewrite each fraction using that denominator. Have them present the
solution to the class and answer questions about their work.

Adding and Subtracting Fractions with Unlike Denominators

USE WITH LESSON 8-4

ACTIVATE PRIOR KNOWLEDGE/BUILD BACKGROUND; EXTEND LANGUAGE

Objective Add and subtract fractions with unlike denominators.

ESL Strategies **Use before** **LEARN** ⏱ 10 MIN

Use ➤ Write the following expression on the board.
Brainstorming

$$\frac{3}{8} + \frac{1}{8}$$

What is the same about these fractions? *(They have the same denominator.)* **How do you add fractions with a common denominator?** *(Add the numerators and write the sum over the common denominator.)* Have a volunteer write the answer on the board. *($\frac{4}{8}$)* Then write the following expression.

$$\frac{1}{4} + \frac{2}{5}$$

What do you notice about these fractions? *(They have different denominators.)* **Can we add them by adding the numerators 1 and 2?** *(No)* **Why?** *(The denominators are not the same.)*

Have Students ➤ Help students understand that they must write equivalent fractions with
Report Back a common denominator before adding. **What is the least common**
in Writing **denominator of $\frac{1}{4}$ and $\frac{2}{5}$?** *(20)* **Now we need to write equivalent fractions with this denominator. What fraction with a denominator of 20 is equal to $\frac{1}{4}$?** *($\frac{5}{20}$)* Write $\frac{5}{20}$ below $\frac{1}{4}$ on the board. **What fraction with a denominator of 20 is equal to $\frac{2}{5}$?** *($\frac{8}{20}$)* Write $+ \frac{8}{20}$ next to $\frac{5}{20}$ on the board. **What is the sum of these two fractions?** *($\frac{13}{20}$)* Write the answer on the board and then write $\frac{2}{4} + \frac{1}{5}$. Have students write out each step in solving the problem.

Understanding Adding and Subtracting Mixed Numbers

USE WITH LESSON 8-5

ACCESS CONTENT

Objective Add and subtract mixed numbers with and without renaming.

Materials *(per pair)* Circle Models (8 sections) (Teaching Tool 51)

Vocabulary Mixed number

ESL Strategies

Use before **LEARN**

⏱ 10 MIN

Use Manipulatives ➤ Write $1\frac{1}{8} + 1\frac{5}{8}$ on the board. **These are called <u>mixed numbers</u>. What are the different parts of each number?** *(A whole number and a fraction)* Arrange students into pairs. Distribute circle models to each pair. **Shade the circle models to show the numbers.** Each partner should model one number. Observe that students shade a whole circle and a fraction of a second circle. **Put your models together. How many whole circles do you have shaded?** *(2 circles)* **How many parts of a circle are shaded?** *(6 parts)* **What fraction of a circle are these parts?** $(\frac{6}{8})$ Write $1\frac{1}{8} + 1\frac{5}{8} = 2\frac{6}{8}$ on the board. **When we add mixed numbers, we can add the whole numbers then add the fractions separately.**

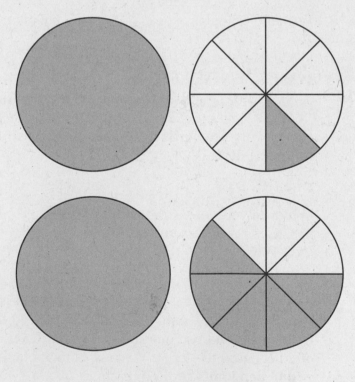

$$1\frac{1}{8} + 1\frac{5}{8} = 2\frac{6}{8}$$

Estimating Sums and Differences of Mixed Numbers

ACTIVATE PRIOR KNOWLEDGE/BUILD BACKGROUND; ACCESS CONTENT

Objective Estimate sums and differences of mixed numbers.

Materials *(per student)* Index card with a mixed number written on it

ESL Strategies | ***Use before*** **LEARN** | ⏱ 5–10 MIN

Connect to Prior Knowledge of Math ➤ **You will be learning to estimate sums and differences of mixed numbers. What is a mixed number?** *(A number that is made up of a whole number and a fraction)* **What is an estimate?** *(An answer that is not the exact answer but is close to it)*

The first step in estimating is to round the mixed number up or down to the nearest whole number. Write $1\frac{2}{3}$ on the board. How do I round this number down? *(Just write the whole number.)* **How do I round this number up?** *(Round up to the next whole number.)* **What is $1\frac{2}{3}$ rounded down?** *(1)* **Rounded up?** *(2)*

Use Small-Group Interactions ➤ Distribute an index card with a mixed number to each student. Have partners take turns explaining to each other how to round their number up and down. Then have students take turns writing their own mixed number for their partners to round.

Adding Mixed Numbers

ACCESS CONTENT

Objective Estimate sums and add mixed numbers.

Materials Measuring cup; water; 3 containers

ESL Strategies | ***Use before*** **LEARN** | ⏱ 10–15 MIN

Use Manipulatives ➤ Measure out $1\frac{1}{4}$ and $1\frac{1}{2}$ c of water and pour each amount into a separate container. Have two volunteers come up and measure the amount of water in each container. Combine the water in another container. Have a volunteer come up and measure the total amount of water. **How much water is there in all?** *($2\frac{3}{4}$ c)* **What number sentence can we write to show how we added the water?** *($1\frac{1}{4}+1\frac{1}{2}=2\frac{3}{4}$)* **What kind of numbers did we add?** *(Mixed numbers)*

Repeat the activity for other measurements such as $1\frac{1}{2}+1\frac{3}{4}$ or $1\frac{1}{3}+1\frac{1}{2}$. Have students estimate the amount of total water before measuring the total.

Subtracting Mixed Numbers

ACCESS CONTENT

USE WITH LESSON **8-8**

Objective Estimate differences and subtract mixed numbers.

Materials Measuring cup; water; 2 containers

ESL Strategies ___ ***Use before*** **LEARN**   🕐 10–15 MIN

Use Manipulatives ➤ Measure out $2\frac{3}{4}$ c of water and pour it into a container. Ask a volunteer to come up and measure the amount. **How much water is in the container?** *($2\frac{3}{4}$ c)* Have two more volunteers come up. One measures and pours out $1\frac{1}{4}$ c of water into another container. The other measures how much water remains in the first container. **How much water is left?** *($1\frac{1}{2}$ c)* **What number sentence can we write to show what we did?** *($2\frac{3}{4} - 1\frac{1}{4} = 1\frac{1}{2}$)* **What kind of numbers did we subtract?** *(Mixed numbers)*

Repeat the activity for other measurements such as $2\frac{1}{4} - 1\frac{1}{4}$ or $3\frac{1}{2} - 1\frac{3}{4}$. Have students estimate the amount of water left in the first container before measuring it.

$2\frac{3}{4} - 1\frac{1}{4} = 1\frac{1}{2}$

Problem-Solving Strategy: Work Backward

EXTEND LANGUAGE

USE WITH LESSON **8-9**

Objective Solve problems that require finding the original times, measurements, or quantities that led to a result that is given.

ESL Strategies ___ ***Use before*** **LEARN**   🕐 10 MIN

Have Students ➤ Divide students into small groups and present this problem. **A train leaves a**
Report Back   **station and travels for 4 hours 32 minutes before arriving at 6:05 PM.**
Orally

Find the time the train left the station, and show your solution to the class. *(1:33 PM)* As groups present their solutions, guide them to the understanding that problems which present the situation at the "end" can often be solved by working backwards to the beginning.

Challenge groups to work backwards to solve the following problem. **Macie collected candy on Halloween. She started eating it on November 1 and ate $\frac{1}{2}$ of what she had plus 1 piece each day. She ate the last piece on November 7. How many pieces of candy did she collect in all?** Do not give students the answer, but encourage them to discuss their solutions until they agree on the "correct" one. *(Macie started with 190 pieces of candy.)*

Date	Candy	Date	Candy
11/1	190 - (95 + 1) = 94	11/5	10 - (5 + 1) = 4
11/2	94 - (47 + 1) = 46	11/6	4 - (2 + 1) = 1
11/3	46 - (23 + 1) = 22	11/7	ate the last piece
11/4	22 - (11 + 1) = 10		

Multiplying Fractions by Whole Numbers

USE WITH LESSON 8-10

ACCESS CONTENT; EXTEND LANGUAGE

Objective Use models or mental math to find fractions of whole numbers.

Materials *(per pair)* Number cube labeled 12, 12, 24, 24, 36, 36; number cube labeled $\frac{1}{2}, \frac{1}{3}, \frac{1}{4}, \frac{2}{3}, \frac{3}{4}, \frac{5}{6}$

ESL Strategies   *Use before* **CHECK** ✓   ⏱ 10 MIN

Use Small-Group Interactions ➤ Arrange students into pairs. Give each pair a set of number cubes. One partner tosses a number cube labeled with whole numbers, and the other tosses a number cube labeled with fractions. Then have partners write a number sentence that shows the multiplication of the fraction and whole number. Direct students to generate a list of four different problems by tossing the number cubes at least three more times. **Work together to solve the four problems.**

Have Students Report Back Orally ➤ When students have correctly solved the problems, ask them to choose and present one of their solutions to the class.

$\frac{1}{4} \times 12 = 3;$

$\frac{2}{3} \times 36 = 24;$

$\frac{5}{6} \times 24 = 20;$

$\frac{1}{3} \times 24 = 8$

Estimating Products of Fractions

ACTIVATE PRIOR KNOWLEDGE/BUILD BACKGROUND; ACCESS CONTENT

Objective Use compatible numbers and mental math to estimate the product of a whole number and a fraction.

Materials *(per student)* Fraction Strips (Teaching Tool 27)

Vocabulary Benchmark

ESL Strategies   *Use before*   **LEARN**   ⏱ 10 MIN

Connect to Prior Knowledge of Math ➤ Write the fractions $\frac{1}{4}$, $\frac{1}{2}$, $\frac{3}{4}$, and 1 on the board. **These fractions are benchmark fractions. Why do we use benchmark fractions?** *(They are easy to multiply.)* **When might you use benchmark fractions?** *(When I want to estimate the answer to a problem)*

Use Manipulatives ➤ Direct students' attention to the fractions written on the board. **Suppose you want to estimate $\frac{5}{8} \times 12$. You can use a benchmark fraction in place of $\frac{5}{8}$.** Have students use fraction strips to compare $\frac{5}{8}$ to each of the benchmark fractions. **Which fraction strip is closest in length to $\frac{5}{8}$?** *(The strip for $\frac{1}{2}$)* **What do you estimate $\frac{5}{8} \times 12$ to be?** *(6)* Repeat the activity so that students match the other benchmark fractions on the board with the fractions $\frac{1}{6}$ *($\frac{1}{4}$)*, $\frac{4}{5}$ *($\frac{3}{4}$)*, and $\frac{7}{8}$ *(1)*. Have students estimate the product of each fraction and 12 using the benchmark fractions. *(3, 9, 12)*

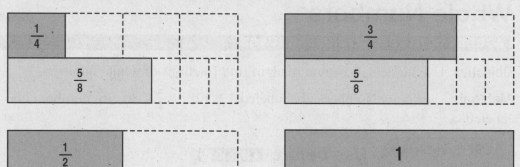

Multiplying Fractions

ACCESS CONTENT

Objective Use models or paper and pencil to multiply fractions.

Materials *(per student)* paper, blue and yellow crayons, ruler

ESL Strategies   *Use before*   **LEARN**   ⏱ 10 MIN

Use Demonstration ➤ Write $\frac{3}{4} \times \frac{1}{3}$ on the board. **Let's model multiplying a fraction by a fraction.** Model $\frac{3}{4}$ by drawing 4 vertical lines on paper and shading

3 sections blue. Have students make the models on their papers. **Now let's model $\frac{1}{3}$. Draw horizontal lines to divide the paper into thirds and shade one section yellow.** Model this step for students if necessary.

The number of green (overlap) sections tells you the numerator of the product. How many green sections are there? *(3)* **The total sections tell the denominator of the product. How many total sections are there?** *(12)* **What is the product of $\frac{3}{4} \times \frac{1}{3}$?** *($\frac{3}{12}$)* **Repeat the activity for $\frac{1}{3} \times \frac{1}{2}$. What is the product of $\frac{1}{3}$ and $\frac{1}{2}$? How do you know?** *($\frac{1}{6}$; There are 6 total sections in the model and 1 section of overlap.)*

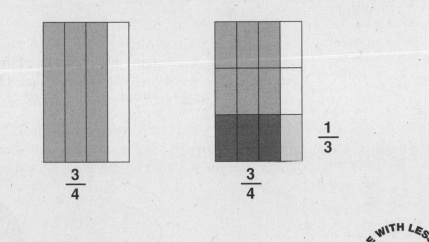

Multiplying Mixed Numbers

USE WITH LESSON 8-13

EXTEND LANGUAGE; ACCESS CONTENT

Objective Multiply mixed numbers.

ESL Strategies *Use before* **LEARN**   ⏲ 5–10 MIN

Focus on Meaning ➤ **Before you multiply a mixed number, you must change it to an improper fraction. A proper fraction has a numerator smaller than its denominator. What do you think an improper fraction is?** *(A fraction with a numerator larger than its denominator)* **Write $\frac{5}{8}$ and $\frac{8}{5}$ on the board. Which fraction is proper?** *($\frac{5}{8}$)* **Improper?** *($\frac{8}{5}$)*

Use ➤
Demonstration **Write $2\frac{1}{4} =$ ___ on the board. Let us change this mixed number to an improper fraction. First we multiply the whole number by the denominator. What is 2×4?** *(8)* **Write 8 in the numerator of the improper fraction. Next, we add 8 and the numerator of the mixed number. Write + 1 next to 8. What is the numerator of the improper fraction?** *(9)* **Write = 9 in the numerator. Finally, we move the denominator over. Write 4 in the denominator. The mixed number 2 1\4 is the same as the improper fraction $\frac{9}{4}$.** Repeat with other mixed numbers and have students tell you what to do.

Understanding Division with Fractions

ACCESS CONTENT

Objective Use models or mental math to divide fractions.

Materials (*per pair*) 4 index cards; Circle Models (divided into 3 sections) (Teaching Tool 51); scissors

ESL Strategies

Use before LEARN

5–10 MIN

Use Manipulatives ➤ Divide the class into pairs and distribute index cards to each pair. **How many cards do you have in all?** (*4 cards*) Have students cut each of the 4 cards in half. **How many halves do you have in all?** (*8 halves*) **When you cut, or divide, the 4 cards in half, you get 8 halves. How can we show this as a number sentence?** ($4 \div \frac{1}{2} = 8$) Write $4 \div \frac{1}{2} = 8$ on the board.

Use Small-Group Interactions ➤ Have students repeat the activity with Circle Models to find $2 \div \frac{1}{3}$. **How many thirds are in 2?** (*6 thirds*) **Explain your answer.** (*Sample answer: When I cut the 2 circles into thirds, I get 6 pieces in all.*)

Problem-Solving Skill: Choose an Operation

ACTIVATE PRIOR KNOWLEDGE/BUILD BACKGROUND; EXTEND LANGUAGE

Objective Solve a problem by choosing an operation.

Materials Slips of paper

ESL Strategies

Use before CHECK ✓

10 MIN

Connect to Prior Knowledge of Math ➤ Display four word problems such as the ones below on the board. Each problem should require one of the four operations—addition, subtraction, multiplication, or division—to solve. **One of these problems can be solved by adding. Which one is it? What language cues helped you to decide?** (*Sample answer: The problem about the recipe; The words "in all" told me to find the total by adding.*) Write "addition" and + next to that problem. Repeat for the other problems.

Write one operation symbol on separate slips of paper. Pass out a slip of paper to each student. **Write a problem that can be solved using the operation on your paper.** Then direct students to trade problems, solve them, and check one another's work. **Which operation did you use to solve your problem?**

Have Students ➤ **What cues helped you to decide?** *(Answers will vary.)*
Report Back
in Writing

$\frac{1}{3}$ of the fish in a tank are guppies. There are 24 fish.
How many are guppies?

Gil has 4 pounds of clay. He uses $1\frac{3}{4}$ pounds.
How many pounds are left?

Each staircase in a 12-floor building has 7 steps.
How many steps are in the building?

A recipe uses $\frac{1}{2}$ c. of cream and $1\frac{3}{4}$ c. of milk.
How much liquid is needed in all?

Problem-Solving Applications: Shoreline Animals

USE WITH LESSON
8-16

ACCESS CONTENT; EXTEND LANGUAGE

Objective Review and apply key concepts, skills, and strategies learned in this and previous chapters.

Language Goal To help students use the language of fraction operations.

Materials *(per pair)* 4-sections spinner labeled $+$, $-$, $\times$, $\div$; index cards with fractions $\frac{1}{2}$, $\frac{1}{3}$, $\frac{1}{4}$, $\frac{2}{3}$, $\frac{2}{5}$, $\frac{3}{4}$, $\frac{3}{5}$, $\frac{4}{5}$, one on each card; paper and pencil

ESL Strategies ➤ **Use before CHECK ✓**   ⏱ 10 MIN

Use Small-Group ➤ Shuffle and place the cards face down. Have each partner pick a card and
Interactions spin the spinner. **What symbol did you land on? Add, subtract, multiply, or divide the fractions on the two cards using that operation.**

Have Students ➤ Have partners present their solutions to each other. *(Sample answer: I*
Report Back *subtracted $\frac{2}{3} - \frac{1}{2}$. The least common denominator is 6 so I wrote $\frac{2}{3}$ as the*
Orally *equivalent fraction $\frac{4}{6}$ and $\frac{1}{2}$ as the equivalent fraction $\frac{3}{6}$. I then subtracted the numerators $4 - 3 = 1$ and wrote that difference over the common denominator, 6. The answer is $\frac{1}{6}$.)* **Do you agree with your partner's answer? Does it make sense? Do you have any questions about it?** Give partners an opportunity to discuss each other's solutions. Then have students draw new cards, spin again, and repeat the activity.

Customary Units of Length

ACCESS CONTENT

USE WITH LESSON 9-1

Objective Change between one customary unit of length and another, and add and subtract customary units of length.

Materials *(per group)* Ruler; yardstick; yarn or string; scissors

ESL Strategies *Use before* **LEARN**   ⏱ 10 MIN

Use Gestures ➤ **What are some units we use to measure length in the United States?** *(Inches, feet, yards, and so on)* **About how long is an inch? Show me with your hands or fingers.** Show a length of 1 inch between your thumb and forefinger and say: **This length is about 1 inch.** Repeat for 1 foot and 1 yard.

Use Real Objects ➤ Have small groups of students work together to measure and cut a length of yarn 1 foot long. **How many inches long is the yarn? Measure to find out.** *(12 in.)* Write "1 foot = 12 inches" on the board. **How many inches are in 1 foot?** *(12)*

Have small groups of students work together to measure and cut a length of yarn 1 yard long. **How many feet long is the yarn? Measure to find out.** *(3 feet)* **How many inches long is the yarn? Measure to find out.** *(36 in.)* Write "1 yard = 3 feet = 36 inches" on the board. **How many feet are in 1 yard?** *(3)* **How many inches are in 1 yard?** *(36)*

1 foot = 12 inches

1 yard = 3 feet = 36 inches

Measuring with Fractions of an Inch

ACCESS CONTENT

USE WITH LESSON 9-2

Objective Measure and draw lengths to the nearest inch, quarter inch, and eighth inch.

Materials *(per student)* Customary rulers

Use before LEARN

Use Real Objects ➤ Distribute a ruler to each student. **Find the 1 in. mark on the ruler. Point to it with your finger, then describe where it is.** *(The long mark shown with the number 1)* **In this lesson, you will learn to measure to the nearest** $\frac{1}{2}$, $\frac{1}{4}$, **and** $\frac{1}{8}$ **in. These measurements are all parts of an inch. Let's find the** $\frac{1}{2}$ **in. mark on the ruler.** Have students point to the mark on their rulers. **Why do you think this is the** $\frac{1}{2}$ **in. mark?** *(Sample answer: It is halfway between 0 and 1 in.)* **The** $\frac{1}{4}$ **in. mark is between 0 and** $\frac{1}{2}$. **Point to it on your ruler.** Repeat for the $\frac{1}{8}$ in. mark. Ask students to explain in their own words how the marks change with each measurement. *(The marks get shorter for smaller fractions of an inch.)* Show students that $\frac{1}{2}$, $\frac{1}{4}$, and $\frac{1}{8}$ in. marks are all along an inch ruler.

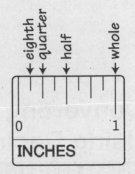

Metric Units of Length

EXTEND LANGUAGE

USE WITH LESSON
9-3

Objective Choose the most appropriate metric unit of length, and measure lengths to the nearest centimeter and millimeter.

Materials Meterstick

Vocabulary Meter

Use before LEARN   ⏱ 10 MIN

Focus on Form ➤ **You can measure length in metric units. The simple metric unit of length is the** <u>meter</u>. Display a meterstick. **Other common metric units are the millimeter, centimeter, and kilometer.** Write the words "millimeter," "centimeter," and "kilometer" on the board. Point to each word as you slowly read it aloud. Ask students to repeat each word after you. **How are all these words similar?** *(They all have the word* meter *in them.)*

You know that a prefix is a group of letters that is added to the beginning of a word. Underline the prefixes *milli-, centi-,* and *kilo-* in each of the corresponding words that you noted on the board. **The prefixes** *milli-, centi-,* **and** *kilo-* **tell you what part of a meter each unit is.** Display a chart like the one below. **Is a millimeter longer or shorter than a meter?** *(Shorter)* **How many millimeters equals 1 meter?** *(1,000)* **What part of a meter is a millimeter?** $(\frac{1}{1,000})$ Repeat the questions for centimeter. **How many meters are in a kilometer?** *(1,000)* **What part of a kilometer is a meter?** $(\frac{1}{1,000})$ Be sure students understand that 1 millimeter and 1 centimeter are fractions of and are smaller than 1 meter. However, 1 meter is a fraction of and is smaller than 1 kilometer.

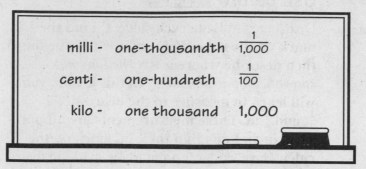

milli - one-thousandth $\frac{1}{1,000}$

centi - one-hundreth $\frac{1}{100}$

kilo - one thousand 1,000

Converting Metric Units Using Decimals

USE WITH LESSON
9-4

ACCESS CONTENT; EXTEND LANGUAGE

Objective Change among measurements in metric units of length.

Materials *(per student)* 2 Place-Value Charts for thousands to thousandths (Teaching Tool 1)

ESL Strategies

Use before LEARN
⏱ 10 MIN

Use ➤
Graphic Organizers

Have students write the titles for thousands to thousandths in a place-value chart. **Our number system and the metric system are both based on the number 10. How many tens are in one hundred?** *(10)* **How many hundreds are in one thousand?** *(10)* **We use the same idea when we change from one metric unit to another.** Help students complete a second chart for metric units. **What is the simple metric unit of length?** *(Meter)* **Write "meter" in the ones place. How many meters are in a kilometer?** *(1,000)* **Where should you write kilometer?** *(In the thousands place)* **Hectometer?** *(Hundreds place)* **Dekameter?** *(Tens place)* **Decimeter?** *(Tenths place)* **Centimeter?** *(Hundredths place)* **Millimeter?** *(Thousandths place).* **We can use a chart like this to show how different metric units are related.**

Have Students ➤
Report Back
Orally

Divide students into pairs or small groups. Ask each group its own different question such as, "How many times larger is a meter than a centimeter?" *(100)* Have the group use the chart to answer the question. Ask each group to explain its answer to the class.

kilometer	hectometer	dekameter	meter	.	decimeter	centimeter	millimeter
				.			

Finding Perimeter

USE WITH LESSON 9-5

ACCESS CONTENT

Objective Find the perimeters of polygons.

Vocabulary Perimeter

Perimeter

ESL Strategies

Use before LEARN

⏱ 5 MIN

Use Demonstration ➤ Write "<u>perimeter</u>" on the board and draw a square, a triangle, and an octagon. **The *perimeter* of a figure is the distance around the edge or outside of the figure.** Trace the perimeter of the square with a pointer or your finger and say, **This is the perimeter of the square.** Repeat for the other polygons.

Use Gestures ➤ **Now you try it. Trace the perimeter of your desk with your finger.** Check that students correctly trace the perimeter, then repeat for a notebook, an index card, ruler, or another objects students keep in their desks.

Finding Circumference

USE WITH LESSON 9-6

ACTIVATE PRIOR KNOWLEDGE/BUILD BACKGROUND; EXTEND LANGUAGE

Objective Find the circumference of a circle by using models and by using a formula.

Materials Yarn or string

Vocabulary Circumference

ESL Strategies

Use before LEARN

⏱ 5 MIN

Connect to Prior Knowledge of Math ➤ **What is the perimeter of a shape or object?** *(The distance around the edge or outside of the figure)* Have students make a circle with the yarn. **Trace the perimeter of the circle with your finger.**

Focus on Form ➤ **The perimeter of a circle has a special name, is called the <u>circumference</u>.** Write the words "circle" and "circumference" on the board. Slowly say both words out loud as you emphasize the beginning letters *circ-*. **How are the words circle and circumference similar?** *(They both begin with the letters circ-.)* **How can you remember that the word *circumference* of a circle describes the outside of a circle?** *(Sample answer: I can remember that circumference begins with the same letters as circle.)*

Finding Area

USE WITH LESSON 9-7

Objective Find the area of irregular shapes by counting square units.

Materials Paper; markers; colored chalk; *(per student)* dot paper with irregular shapes drawn on it

Vocabulary Area

ESL Strategies

Use before LEARN

🕐 10–15 MIN

Use ➤
Demonstration
Before beginning the lesson, prepare a piece of dot paper to copy for each student. Trace or draw irregular shapes on the dot paper. Using the dots as guides, students will be expected to find the <u>area</u> of these shapes in square units. First write "area" on the board and draw a square. **In mathematics, *area* is the amount of space that an object covers.** Use colored chalk to shade the square and say, **The shaded part stands for the area of the square.**

Use Pictures ➤
Distribute the dot paper with shapes to each student. **We will measure the area of these shapes using square units. How can we see the number of squares in each figure?** *(Connect the dots to make squares within the shapes. Then count the squares.)* **What if you have leftover space that is only part of a square unit?** *(Estimate the fraction of square unit left over.)* Demonstrate how to do this. Draw and work through an example on the board. **Count how many square units you find in your shapes. Write the area, or number of square units, next to each shape.** As students work, circulate in the room to observe their progress, giving help when it is needed. When students have finished, have volunteers share their answers and explain how they found them. Have students correct their work.

Areas of Squares and Rectangles

USE WITH LESSON 9-8

Objective Find areas of rectangles and squares by using formulas.

Materials Masking tape; 16 paper squares 1 ft × 1 ft

ESL Strategies

Use before LEARN

🕐 10–15 MIN

Use Real Objects ➤
Use tape to make an outline of a 3 ft × 5 ft rectangle on the floor. **Let's find the area of this rectangle.** Show one of the paper squares. **This square has an area of 1 ft².** Have students lay out paper squares to cover the rectangle, then count them to find the area. **What is the area of the rectangle?** *(15 ft²)*

Have students count the number of squares along the length and width. **How many feet long is the rectangle?** *(5 ft)* **How many feet wide is it?** *(3 ft)* Write the equation "3 feet ____ 5 feet = 15 square feet" on the board. **What operation should you use to complete this equation?**

(Multiplication) Write the multiplication sign in the blank of the equation. **You can multiply the number of squares on the length and width to find the area.** Repeat the activity for a 4 ft × 4 ft square.

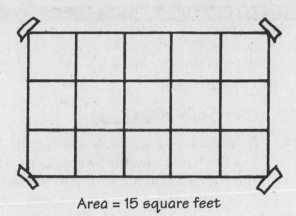

Area = 15 square feet

Areas of Parallelograms

ACTIVATE PRIOR KNOWLEDGE/BUILD BACKGROUND

Objective Find the areas of a parallelogram by using a formula, and find the length when the area and other side length are known.

Materials *(per student)* Dot Paper (Teaching Tool 25); ruler

ESL Strategies | ***Use before*** **LEARN** | ⏱ 10–15 MIN

Connect to Prior Knowledge of Math

Write "parallelogram" on the board. Circle "parallel" in the term. **What are parallel lines?** *(Lines that go on forever without touching)* **What are some objects with parallel lines?** *(Sample answers: Two sides of a ladder, opposite sides of a door)* Draw a parallelogram. **A parallelogram is a 4-sided shape. Why do you think it is called a parallelogram?** *(Opposite sides are parallel.)* Have students use dot paper and a ruler to draw a parallelogram. **How do you know your drawing is a parallelogram?** *(The opposite sides are parallel to each other.)* Circulate in the room to see that students have drawn a parallelogram. **What shapes do we already know that have 2 pairs of opposite sides that are parallel?** *(Square, rectangle)* **Squares and rectangles are special types of parallelograms.**

To find the area of a parallelogram, we use a formula. Write "base × height = area of a parallelogram" on the board. Draw a line in the parallelogram on the board that shows its height. Write "height" and "base" next to the appropriate lines on the board. Have students use their rulers to draw a parallelogram with 2 in. × 1 in. sides. **Use your ruler to find the height. Find the area of the parallelogram in square inches.** Have volunteers share how they solved the problem. Demonstrate the equation on the board so students can check their work.

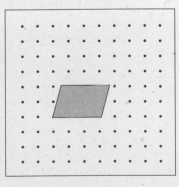

Areas of Triangles

ACCESS CONTENT; EXTEND LANGUAGE

Objective Find the area of a triangle by using a formula, and find a missing length when the area and other dimension are known.

Materials pre-cut paper triangles, rulers

ESL Strategies   *Use before* **LEARN**   10 MIN

Use Small-Group Interactions ➤ Write "area = $\frac{1}{2}$ base $\times$ height" on the board. **The area of a triangle equals $\frac{1}{2}$ of the base times the height. Let's write this formula using symbols to make it easier to remember. What letter can we use to stand for "area?"** Give small groups of students time to choose a symbol and explain their choice to the class. *(Sample answer: We chose a capital letter A because "a" is the first letter in area and we have used the capital letter to stand for area in other formulas.)* **Choose letters for the "base" and "height" and explain your choices.**

Have Students Report Back Orally ➤ Give each group a paper triangle. **Measure the base and height of the triangle, then write the formula for the area using those measurements.** Ask each group to show the class how it measured and wrote the formula.

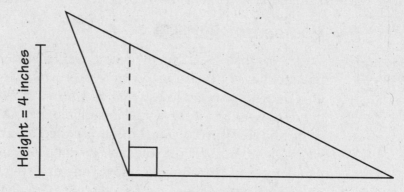

Height = 4 inches

Base = 6 inches

$$A = \frac{1}{2} \times 6 \times 4$$

Problem-Solving Strategy: Draw a Picture

ACCESS CONTENT

Objective Draw pictures that represent the information given in problems.

Materials *(per student)* Inch grid paper; ruler

ESL Strategies | *Use before* **LEARN** | ⏱ 10 MIN

Use Pictures ➤ **One strategy for solving problems is to draw a picture of what you know. This can help you solve problems about perimeter and area. Let's practice using directions to make a picture.** Distribute the grid paper and remind students that each square is 1 in. long. **Draw a rectangle that is 4 in. long and 3 in. wide.** Have partners exchange papers to check each other's work. **Now draw a square that measures 2 in. on each side. Now draw a rectangle that is 1 in. wide. Make the length 2 in. longer than the width.**

Divide the class into pairs. **Now use the pictures to find the perimeter and area of these shapes.** *(Rectangle 4 in. × 3 in.: area = 12 in², perimeter = 14 in.; square 2 in. × 2 in.: area = 4 in², perimeter = 8 in.; rectangle 3 in. × 1 in.: area = 3 in², perimeter = 8 in.)* Encourage students to count to find the perimeter and multiply the length and width to find area of each object.

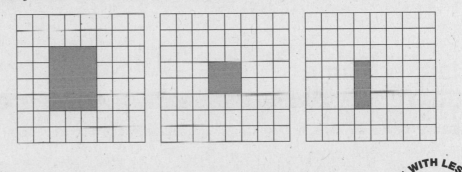

Time

ACTIVATE PRIOR KNOWLEDGE/BUILD BACKGROUND; EXTEND LANGUAGE

Objective Change from one unit of time to another.

Materials *(per group)* Chart paper; tape; markers

ESL Strategies | *Use before* **LEARN** | ⏱ 10 MIN

Connect to Prior Knowledge of Language ➤ **What does the prefix *cent-* mean? Here is a hint: There are 100 centimeters in a meter.** *(Hundred)* **What are some words that have the prefix *cent-*?** *(Centimeter, cent)* **In this lesson, we will use different units of time, including a *century*.** Write the word "century" on the board and invite students to repeat the word after you. **How many years do you think are in a century?** *(100)*

Have Students Report Back in Writing ➤ Write these problems on the board.

$$4 \text{ centuries} = \underline{\hspace{1cm}} \text{ years}$$

$$200 \text{ years} = \underline{\hspace{1cm}} \text{ centuries}$$

Divide the class into groups and give each group chart paper and markers. Have the groups choose one of the problems and work together to write the mathematical steps needed to solve it. When students have finished, display their solutions by taping each group's chart to the board.

> 4 centuries = _____ years
> 4 X 100 = 400
> 4 centuries = 400 years
> We multiplied to find the number of years

Elapsed Time

EXTEND LANGUAGE

USE WITH LESSON
9-13

Objective Given any two of these times, elapsed time, starting time, or ending time, find the third.

Materials *(per pair)* Stopwatch

Vocabulary Elapsed time

ESL Strategies

Use before CHECK ✓

⏱ 5 MIN

Focus on Meaning ➤ Divide the class into pairs and distribute a stopwatch to each. Tell students you want them to start and stop the watch when you say "start" and "stop." Say **Start** and **Stop** at a 10 second interval. **How much time has *elapsed?*** *(10 seconds)* Repeat the activity for different times. **What does *elapsed* mean?** *(Passed or gone by)* **What is <u>elapsed time</u>?** *(The amount of time that passes between a start time and a stop time)*

Temperature

ACCESS CONTENT; ACTIVATE PRIOR KNOWLEDGE/BUILD BACKGROUND

Objective Read temperatures in degrees Fahrenheit and in degrees Celsius on a thermometer with both scales, and give changes in temperature indicating the amount of increase or decrease.

Vocabulary Celsius

ESL Strategies **Use before** **LEARN** 🕐 10 MIN

Use Gestures ➤ Write "hot," "warm," "cool," and "cold" on the board. Ask students to make gestures to show each temperature condition. Students may, for example, shiver to show cold or fan themselves to show hot.

Connect to Prior ➤ Write 0°C, 10°C, 20°C, and 30°C" on the board. **One way to tell**
Knowledge of **temperature is in degrees** Celsius. Point to °C in the temperatures.
Math **This symbol means degrees Celsius.**

What do you notice about the four temperatures I have written on the board? *(They start at zero and increase by 10 degrees Celsius.)* **The words cold, cool, warm, or hot can describe what it feels like when the temperature is at 0°C, 10°C, 20°C, or 30°C. Which word best describes what it feels like when the temperature is at 0°C?** *(Cold)* **How do you know?** *(0°C is the lowest temperature.)* Continue to match the temperatures to the words. Discuss how students can use the guidelines to estimate temperatures in degrees Celsius.

```
 0° C  cold
10° C  cool
20° C  warm
30° C  hot
```

Problem-Solving Skill:
Writing to Explain

EXTEND LANGUAGE; ACCESS CONTENT

Objective Write to explain how a broken ruler can be used to measure.

Materials *(per pair)* ruler with masking tape covering about the first $2\frac{1}{2}$ inches, paper with a $4\frac{3}{8}$ in line on it

ESL Strategies   *Use before*   **LEARN**   ⏱ 10 MIN

Have Students ➤
Report Back
Orally

You have been given a broken ruler. Explain how it is broken. *(Sample answer: You cannot read the numbers or see the marks for the first few inches.)* **You want to measure the length of this line. Work together to make a plan to use the broken ruler to measure it. Explain your plan.** *(Sample answer: We will put the 3-inch mark of the ruler at one end of the line, then read off the mark at the other end. After we subtract 3 inches from that number, we will know the length of the line.)*

Use Real Objects ➤
Use the ruler to find the length of the line. When students correctly find its length, challenge them to work together to draw a line exactly $3\frac{3}{4}$ inches long using the broken ruler.

Problem-Solving Applications:
Statue of Liberty

ACTIVATE PRIOR KNOWLEDGE/BUILD BACKGROUND

Objective Review and apply key concepts, skills, and strategies learned in this and previous chapters.

Materials *(per pair)* Centimeter Grid Paper (Teaching Tool 49); Centimeter Ruler (Teaching Tool 35)

ESL Strategies   *Use before*   **LEARN**   ⏱ 10 MIN

Connect to Prior ➤
Knowledge of
Math

Have small groups of students draw three different rectangles on the grid paper. **Measure and write the length and width of the first rectangle.** *(Sample answer: length 4 cm and width 3 cm)* **What is the area?** *($12\ cm^2$)* **Measure and write the length and width of the second rectangle. What is the area? Measure and write the length and width of the third rectangle. What is the area?**

How does the area of a rectangle relate to its length and width? *(The area of a rectangle is the product of the length and width.)* Write a formula for the area of rectangle, using *l* to stand for the length and *w* to stand for width.

$(A = l \times w)$ Repeat this activity and line of questioning to relate the side of a square to its area $(A = s \times s = s^2)$, the base and height of a parallelogram to its area $(A = b \times h)$, and the base and height of a triangle to its area $(A = \frac{1}{2} b \times h)$.

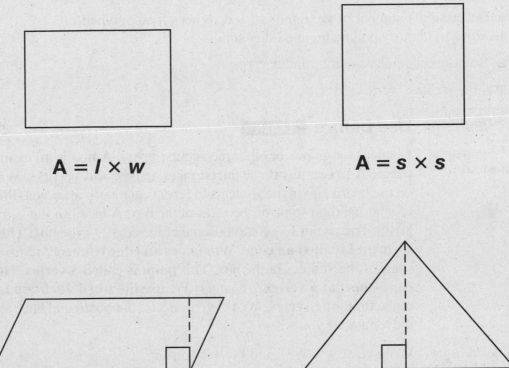

$A = l \times w$

$A = s \times s$

$A = b \times h$

$A = \frac{1}{2} b \times h$

Solid Figures

ACCESS CONTENT

USE WITH LESSON
10-1

Objective Describe the number of faces, edges, and vertices for a polyhedron and use features to identify polyhedra and other solids.

Materials Box or rectangular prism; 3 index cards

Vocabulary Prism, face, vertex, edge

ESL Strategies | **Use before** LEARN | 🕐 5–10 MIN

Use Demonstration ➤ Display a large box or other rectangular <u>prism</u>. **A box is an example of a prism. A prism has three parts: <u>faces</u>, <u>edges</u>, and <u>vertices</u>.** Write the terms on the board and invite students to repeat each term after you. Place the palm of your hand on some of the faces of the box. A face is a flat surface on a prism. Trace your finger along some of the edges of the box. **This line segment is called an edge. What does an edge connect?** *(2 faces)* Point to some of the vertices of the box. **This point is called a vertex. How many edges meet at a vertex?** *(3 edges)* **We use the word *vertices* to talk about more than one vertex.** Write "vertices" on the board and have students repeat the term after you.

Use Gestures ➤ Write "face," "edge," and "vertex" on separate index cards. Shuffle the cards facedown and have a volunteer select one and read the term to the class. Ask the student to show the class the part of the box written on the selected index card. Continue this activity with other volunteers until students are comfortable identifying these parts of a prism.

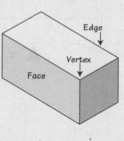

Views of Solid Figures

ACCESS CONTENT

USE WITH LESSON
10-2

Objective Identify solids from their nets, and draw front, top and side views of solids.

Materials *(per group)* Net for Cone (Teaching Tool 41); Net for Cylinder (Teaching Tool 43); Net for Rectangular Prism (Teaching Tool 44); Net for Square Pyramid (Teaching Tool 46); tape

Vocabulary Net

Use before CHECK ✓   ◔ 10–15 MIN

Use Manipulatives ➤ Divide the class into groups. Distribute nets for a cone, a cylinder, a rectangular prism, and a square pyramid to each group. Write "cone," "cylinder," "rectangular prism," and "square pyramid" on the board. **We can fold a net to make one of these solid figures.** Ask groups to predict which net will build each of the four figures. **What net do you think will make a (cone, cylinder, prism, square pyramid)?** *(Answers will vary.)* **Why?** *(Sample answer: The net has a circle. I know a cone has a circle for a face.)* **What clues helped you decide?** *(Sample answer: The shapes that make up a net)* Have students build the nets and discuss whether or not their predictions were correct. Then have groups draw front, top, and side views of each of the solid figures and relate their drawings to what the nets looked like before being built. **What do you notice about your drawings and the way the nets originally looked?** *(Sample answer: In one of my drawings of a cone, I have a circle. The net for a cone also has a circle.)*

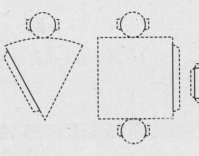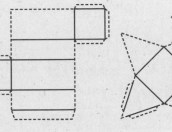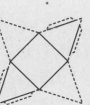

Net for cone   Net for cylinder   Net for rectangualr   Net for square pyramid
                                           prism

Surface Area

USE WITH LESSON
10-3

EXTEND LANGUAGE; ACTIVATE PRIOR KNOWLEDGE/BUILD BACKGROUND

Objective Use a formula to find the surface area of rectangular prisms.

Materials *(per student)* Rectangular prism or net for a cube; tape

Vocabulary Surface area

Use before LEARN   ◔ 5–10 MIN

Focus on Meaning ➤ Write "surface area" on the board. Distribute a rectangular prism or the net for a cube and tape to each student. If students are using a net, have them build it. **Indicate the surface of your desk with your hand.** *(Students should touch the surface of their desk.)* **What is the surface of an object?** *(The outside of the object)* **What is the area of an object?** *(The amount of space an object covers)* **So what do you think the surface area of a solid figure is?** *(The total area of the outside of a figure).*

Use Brainstorming ➤ **How could we find the surface area of this rectangular prism?** *(Find the area of each face, then add each area to find the total.)* Have students brainstorm and share their ideas with the class.

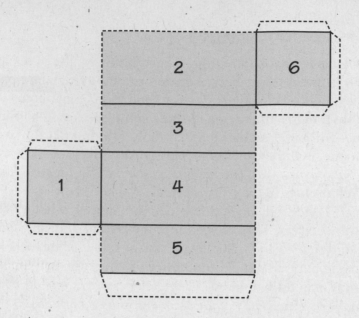

Surface area = Sum of Areas (1 + 2 + 3 + 4 + 5 + 6)

Problem-Solving Strategy: Use Objects

USE WITH LESSON 10-4

ACCESS CONTENT

Objective Use objects to solve a problem that involves finding a pattern.

Materials *(per group)* 60 two-color counters

ESL Strategies **Use before** **LEARN** ⏱ 10 MIN

Use Manipulatives ➤ Draw models of the three triangular numbers (1, 2, and 3) on the board or chart paper, and have students model them using red-side-up counters. **These numbers are called "triangular" numbers. Why do you think they have that name?** *(Sample answer: When you model the number, it forms the shape of a triangle.)* **What patterns do you notice about them?** *(Each row has one more counter than the row above.)* **How many counters are in the first model? the second? the third?** *(1, 3, 6)* **How many counters would you need to model the fourth number?** *(10)* **What pattern do you see in the numbers?** *(I add 2, then 3, then 4 and so on.)* Have groups use counters and/or the pattern to find the number of counters needed to model the sixth number. *(21)* **Explain how you solved this problem.** *(Sample answer: The counters helped me see the pattern and keep track of the number in each model.)*

Volume

EXTEND LANGUAGE; ACCESS CONTENT

Objective Use cubes and a formula to find the volume of rectangular prisms.

Materials *(per group)* 40 one-inch cubes

ESL Strategies   **Use before** **LEARN**   🕐 10–15 MIN

Focus on Meaning ➤ Have groups of students put together two adjoining rows of five cubes. Then have them stack two more layers on top, with two rows of five cubes in each layer. The resulting prism should be five cubes long, two cubes wide, and three cubes high. **Each of these cubes is 1 inch long on each side. How long is this prism?** *(5 inches)* **What is the width of this prism?** *(2 inches)* **The height of this prism is how tall it is. What is its height?** *(3 inches)* If necessary, point out what each question is referring to. Write "length × width × height = volume of a prism" on the board. **We can use this formula to find the volume of a prism: the length times the width times the height of the prism.** Below the formula, write 5 inches × 2 inches × 3 inches = ___. **What is the volume of the prism that you built?** *(30 in³)*

Use Manipulatives ➤ Have each group build its own prisms and identify the length, width, and height of each one. Then have students solve for the volume of each prism.

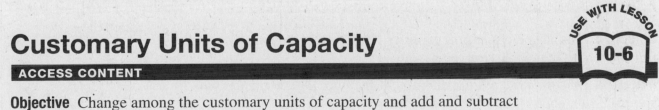

Customary Units of Capacity

ACCESS CONTENT

Objective Change among the customary units of capacity and add and subtract customary units of capacity.

Materials *(per group)* Cup, pint, quart, and gallon containers; water

Vocabulary Cup, pint, quart, gallon

Use before `LEARN`   ⏱ 10 MIN

Use Real Objects ➤ Write the following statements on the board.

1 pint = ___ cups

1 quart = ___ pints

1 gallon = ___ quarts

Point to each term as you say, **You can use <u>cups</u>, <u>pints</u>, <u>quarts</u>, and <u>gallons</u> to measure capacity, or the amount of liquid in a container. Let us figure out how these units are related.** Divide the class into groups and give each group cup, pint, quart, and gallon containers. Have each group use the cup container to fill the pint container with water. **How many cups are in 1 pint?** *(2 cups)* Have a volunteer write the answer on the board. Then have each group find out how many pints are in a quart and how many quarts are in a gallon using the same process. *(2 pint = 1 quart; 4 quart = 1 gallon)* Ask volunteers to fill in the information on the board.

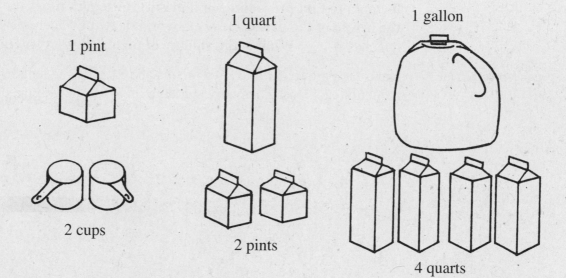

1 pint

2 cups

1 quart

2 pints

1 gallon

4 quarts

Metric Units of Capacity

USE WITH LESSON
10-7

`ACTIVATE PRIOR KNOWLEDGE/BUILD BACKGROUND; ACCESS CONTENT`

Objective Estimate and measure capacity using metric measures, and change millimeters to liters and vice versa.

Materials *(per group)* eyedropper; small paper cup; liter container; plastic spoon; 2-liter soda bottle; 1-gallon container

Vocabulary Milliliter, liter

Connect to Prior ➤ **The amount of liquid that a container can hold is its capacity. Common
Experiences   metric units of capacity are the <u>milliliter</u> and <u>liter</u>.** Show the eyedropper
and squeeze out one drop of water. **This drop is about one milliliter.** Show
the liter container. **This container holds one liter, or 1,000 milliliters.**

Use Real Objects ➤ **How many milliliters do you think the spoon will hold?** Have groups
make and write an estimate, then use the eyedropper to measure. Have them
repeat the activity for the paper cup. **How many liters do you think the
bottle will hold?** Have groups make and write an estimate, then use the liter
container to measure. Have them repeat the activity for the gallon container.

A liter container holds about the same as a quart container.

Customary Units of Weight

USE WITH LESSON
10-8

ACCESS CONTENT

Objective Change between customary units of weight, and add and subtract
customary units of weight.

Materials *(per group)* Balance; 1 one-pound weight; 20 one-ounce weights

Vocabulary Pound, ounce

ESL Strategies   Use before LEARN   ⏱ 10–15 MIN

Use ➤ **What is weight?** *(How heavy or light an object is)* In the United States, we
Demonstration   often weigh things in <u>ounces</u> and <u>pounds</u>. Write "ounces" and "pounds" on the
board. Pass around the weights and give students an opportunity to feel them.

Use Small-Group ➤ Divide the class into groups and distribute a balance and weights to each.
Interactions   **Hold a one-pound weight in your left hand and a one-ounce weight in
your right hand. About how many ounces do you think equal 1 pound?**
Remind students that their answers should be estimates and not exact
answers. Encourage students to share their estimates with their group. Then
have students put the one-pound weight on the left side of the balance and
enough one-ounce weights on the right to make the balance level. **How
many ounces equal one pound?** *(16 ounces)* **How close were your**

estimates? *(Answers will vary.)* Write "16 ounces = 1 pound" on the board. **If 16 ounces equal 1 pound, how many ounces are in 2 pounds?** *(32 ounces)* **How many ounces are in half a pound?** *(8 ounces)*

Metric Units of Mass

EXTEND LANGUAGE

Objective Estimate and measure mass using metric measures, and change between these measures.

Vocabulary Milligram, gram, kilogram

ESL Strategies   **Use before** **LEARN**   ⏱ 5 MIN

Focus on Form ➤ Write "millimeter," "meter," and "kilometer" on the board. **You have used millimeters, meters, and kilometers to measure length. The prefix *milli*-means $\frac{1}{1,000}$. How many millimeters equal one meter?** *(1,000 millimeters)* **The prefix *kilo-* means 1,000. How many meters equal one kilometer?** *(1,000 meters)* Record the information in a chart on the board, as illustrated below, and have students copy it into their math journals.

Write "milligram," "gram," and "kilogram" in the right-hand column of the chart. **You can measure mass, or weight, using the units milligram, gram, and kilogram. Think about the prefixes. What fraction of a gram is one milligram?** *($\frac{1}{1,000}$)* **How many milligrams equal one gram?** *(1,000 milligrams)* **How many grams are in one kilogram?** *(1,000 grams)*

millimeter	$\frac{1}{1,000}$	milligram
meter	1	gram
kilometer	1,000	kilogram

Problem-Solving Skill: Exact Answer or Estimate

ACCESS CONTENT

Objective Give an exact answer or an estimate on what the problem asks.

Materials Glass jar with 6 paper clips; glass jar with about 75 clips; *(per pair)*
paper clips

ESL Strategies   **Use before** **LEARN**   ⏱ 10 MIN

Use Demonstration ➤ Invite students to examine closely the jar with six paper clips. How many **paper clips are in this jar?** *(6 paper clips)* **How do you know?** *(I counted each one.)* **You have given an exact answer.** Invite students to examine closely the jar with about 75 paper clips and ask, **How many paper clips are in this jar?** *(Answers will vary.)* **How do you know?** *(Sample answer: There seem to be about that many paper clips.)* **If I say there are about 75 paper clips in this jar, I have made an estimate. I cannot count every single paper clip just by looking at the jar, so I made a careful guess and rounded the amount.**

Use ➤ Arrange students into pairs. One student makes a small pile and a large pile
Peer Questioning of paper clips. The student asks his or her partner how many paper clips are in each pile. The partner answers using the term *exact* or *estimate*. Then partners switch roles and repeat the activity, using different numbers of paper clips in each pile.

Problem-Solving Applications:
Water

ACCESS CONTENT

Objective Review and apply key concepts, skills, and strategies learned in this and previous chapters.

Materials *(per pair)* 2 cardboard boxes in different sizes; Rulers (Centimeter, Meter Stick) (Teaching Tool 35)

ESL Strategies **Use before** **LEARN** ⏱ 10 MIN

Use Real Objects ➤ Have students work together to measure and label the length, width, and height of the first box in centimeters. Assign one student to find the surface area and the other to find the volume of the box. **After you solve your problem, explain to your partner how you found the answer.** *(Surface area: find the area of each of the 6 faces by multiplying the length and width of each face, then add the 6 areas; Volume: multiply the length times the width times the height.)* **What is the surface area? What is the volume?** Have students repeat the activity with the second box. Assign the student who found the surface area to find the volume, and vice versa.

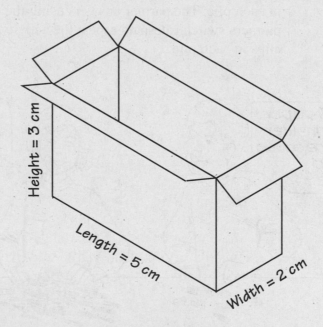

Height = 3 cm

Length = 5 cm

Width = 2 cm

Understanding Ratios

ACCESS CONTENT

Objective Read and write ratios for various kinds of comparisons, and tell which situation represents a ratio that is a fraction (part-whole) and which represents a ratio that is not a fraction.

Materials *(per pair)* 10 Two-color counters; paper bag

ESL Strategies | *Use before* **LEARN**   ⏱ 5–10 MIN

Use Manipulatives ➤ Draw a three-column chart on the board. Write the following labels at the top of each column: "Number of Red Counters," "Number of Yellow Counters," "Total Number of Counters." Divide the class into pairs. Have each pair copy the chart on a sheet of paper. Ask the students to pick a handful of counters from the bag and put them on the desk. **How many red counters are there? How many yellow counters? How many counters in all?** Have students complete the chart. **A ratio is a relationship between two amounts. Sometimes it can relate a part of something to another part of the same thing. Sometimes it can relate a part to a whole. How can you show the relationship of a part to a whole?** *(With a fraction)* **Compare the number of red counters to the total number of counters. Write the comparison as a fraction.** *(Sample answer: There are 5 red and 8 total counters. The fraction is $\frac{5}{8}$.)* **Compare the yellow to the total number of counters. Write the comparison as a fraction.** *(Sample answer: There are 3 yellow and 8 total counters. The fraction is $\frac{3}{8}$.)* **Compare the number of yellow to red counters.** *(Sample answer: There are 3 yellow and 5 red counters.)* **Can you write this ratio as a fraction?** *(No)* **Why not?** *(Because it does not show the relationship of a part to a whole)*

Use Peer Questioning ➤ Direct students to return the counters to the bag and repeat the activity. Have them complete the chart and then take turns asking and answering questions that compare the red to total, yellow to total, and red to yellow counters.

Equal Ratios

ACCESS CONTENT

Objective Use a table to generate equal ratios, write equal ratios, and tell if two ratios form a proportion.

Materials *(per group)* Measuring cup; water; clear container; food coloring (one color); index cards

Vocabulary Equal ratios

ESL Strategies *Use before* **LEARN** ⏱ 10 MIN

Use Real Objects ➤ Divide students into 4 groups and give each group one of the following recipes, written on a card.

Mix 3 drops of food coloring with 1 cup of water.

Mix 6 drops of food coloring with 2 cups of water.

Mix 9 drops of food coloring with 3 cups of water.

Mix 12 drops of food coloring with 4 cups of water.

Have each group prepare its recipe, then set the 4 containers on a table with the cards next to them. **How are the containers alike? How are they different?** *(Sample answer: Each container has the same shade of blue water in it. The amount of water in each container is different.)* **These containers show <u>equal ratios</u> of food coloring to water if the amount of food coloring for each cup of water is the same in all four containers. Do these containers show equal ratios of food coloring to water?** *(Yes)* **How can you tell?** *(The water in each container is the same shade, or darkness.)* Write 3:1, 6:2, 9:3, and 12:4 on the board. **These are the ratios the groups used to make the water. What can you conclude about these ratios?** *(Sample answer: The numbers are different, but they show equal ratios, or equal parts, of food coloring to water.)*

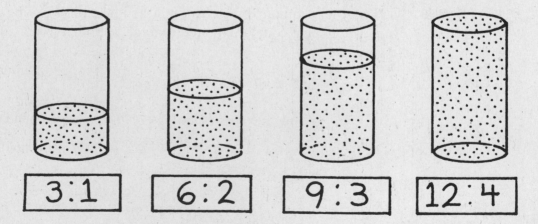

Graphs of Equal Ratios

ACTIVATE PRIOR KNOWLEDGE/BUILD BACKGROUND; EXTEND LANGUAGE

Objective Generate a table of equal ratios and graph the ordered pairs.

ESL Strategies   *Use before* **LEARN**   ⏱ 5 MIN

Connect to Prior Knowledge of Math ➤ Ask students to find a line graph in the Student Book. **How do you know that this graph is a line graph?** *(Sample answer: The data is connected by a line segment.)* Have students quiz each other on the properties of line graphs. Guide them to ask how points are found and how information can be read from the graph.

Have Students Report Back in Writing ➤ **On the trip to the amusement park, every student gets 4 ride tickets. How many tickets do we need for 2 students?** *(8)* Have students continue this calculation out to 10 students. Then have small groups make posters that show a line graph of this data. Display the posters around the classroom and discuss the line graphs. **What does the graph look like?** *(A straight line)* **Do all the points show equal ratios?** *(Yes)* **How do you know?** *(Each point to the right of the graph shows 4 more tickets for every extra student.)*

Rates

ACTIVATE PRIOR KNOWLEDGE/BUILD BACKGROUND; EXTEND LANGUAGE

Objective Read and write rates, and change a rate to a unit rate.

Vocabulary Rate

ESL Strategies   *Use before* **LEARN**   ⏱ 10 MIN

Use Role Playing ➤ Ask two volunteers to perform a skit. Assign one to play a baby-sitter and one to play a parent. **I want you to discuss a price to pay the baby-sitter each hour. The baby-sitter starts by saying how much he or she wants to make per hour. The parent then says how much he or she is willing to give the baby-sitter.** Guide students as they negotiate an hourly <u>rate</u>, then write it on the board. Repeat the activity for different negotiations as you read each of the scenarios below.

Three engineers discuss how many miles per hour cars can travel on a bridge.

Two store clerks discuss how many dollars a pound of candy costs.

Two coaches discuss how many days the team should practice each week.

These expressions are rates. **Rates compare two amounts with different units. What are the units in the baby-sitter's price?** *(Dollars and hours)* **What are the units of the car's speed?** *(Miles and hours)* **What are the units in the candy price?** *(Dollars and pounds)* **What are the units in the team schedule?** *(Days and weeks)* **Can you think of other rates?** *(Sample answers: 20 miles per gallon, 4 students to each table, and so on)*

$5 per hour
40 miles per hour
$2.00 per hour
3 practices each day

Problem-Solving Strategy: Make a Table

USE WITH LESSON

11-5

ACTIVATE PRIOR KNOWLEDGE/BUILD BACKGROUND; ACCESS CONTENT

Objective Make tables and use them to solve word problems.

Materials 3 erasers; 2 books; 4 pencils; 3 index cards

ESL Strategies **_Use before_** **LEARN**   ⏱ 10 MIN

Use Brainstorming ➤ Set up a "store" stocked with erasers, books, and pencils. Use index cards to show the prices: $2 per eraser, $8 per book, and $1 per pencil. **How much will it cost to buy all of these things? Talk about how you can find the total cost.** Allow students time to discuss strategies.

Use Graphic ➤ Draw a table like the one below. **You can use a table to organize**
Organizers **information.** Write "eraser" in the first column. **How many erasers are there?** *(3)* **How much does each one cost?** *($2)* **How can we find the total cost of the erasers?** *(Multiply 3 × $2.)* **What is the total?** *($6)* Have student volunteers ask similar questions to the class to finish filling in the table. **How do you find the total cost of everything listed in the table?** *(Add the totals for each object.)* **What is the total?** *($26)* **How did making a table help you solve this problem?** *(Sample answer: It helped me solve the problem one step at a time and helped keep the information organized.)*

Object	Number	Cost	Total Cost
eraser	3	$2	$6
book	2	$8	$16
pencil	4	$1	$4

Scale Drawings

ACCESS CONTENT; EXTEND LANGUAGE

Objective Create scale drawings.

Materials Centimeter Grid Paper (Teaching Tool 49); ruler

Vocabulary Scale drawing

 **ESL Strategies** *Use before* **CHECK ✓**   ⏱ 5 MIN

Use Small-Group Interactions ➤ Assign students to small groups. Let each group choose a simple object such as a desk to use for a <u>scale drawing</u>. **Work together to make a scale drawing of your object. Remember that you must follow these steps.** Write the steps below on the board. Invite different volunteers to read aloud each step.

      1. Measure the object.

      2. Choose a scale.

      3. Make the drawing.

      4. Write the scale and label the drawing.

Have Students Report Back Orally ➤ Ask each group to present its scale drawing and explain how it was created. **What scale did you use? Why did you choose that scale?** *(Sample answer: We used 1 cm on the drawing to stand for 10 cm of the object. We chose that scale because we could make a drawing that filled the paper.)*

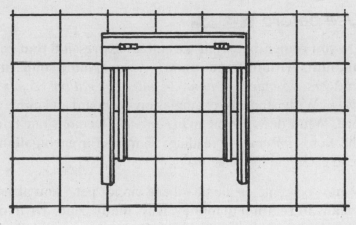

10 cm = 1 cm

Problem-Solving Skill: Writing to Explain

USE WITH LESSON 11-7

ACTIVATE PRIOR KNOWLEDGE/BUILD BACKGROUND

Objective Write to explain a prediction.

Materials *(per pair)* 4 each red, blue, yellow connecting cubes; opaque bag

ESL Strategies   *Use before* **LEARN**   10 MIN

Use Simulation ➤ Have one partner put any 4 cubes into the bag, showing the other partner the colors selected. **If you pick one cube from the bag, what color do you think it will be? How sure are you? Explain.** *(Sample answer: I am pretty sure the cube will be blue because my partner put 3 blue and 1 red cube in the bag. Most of the cubes are blue.)* Have partners select a cube to test the prediction, then alternate roles and repeat the activity with 4 new cubes several times.

Understanding Percent

USE WITH LESSON 11-8

EXTEND LANGUAGE

Objective Write a percent for a given situation on a 100-grid, and create a 100-grid that shows various percents.

Vocabulary Percent

ESL Strategies   *Use before* **LEARN**   5 MIN

Focus on Meaning ➤ **Do you remember what we call an expression that compares two amounts with different units?** *(A rate)* **Name some rates.** *(Sample answers: 55 miles per hour, 24 miles per gallon, $5 per pound, 5 times per week)* Write students' examples on the board and circle the word *per* in each one. **What does *per* mean?** *(For each)* Demonstrate how to replace *per* with the words *for each* by reading: **55 miles for each gallon.** Have volunteers read each rate the same way.

Write "<u>percent</u>" on the board and circle "per." **You already know what *cent* means in relation to money. How many cents are in one dollar?** *(100)* *Cent* **is also sometimes a part of a bigger word. When *cent* is a word part, it stands for the number 100. Put the word parts *per* and *cent* together. What does *percent* mean?** *(Per hundred, for each hundred)* **If I have 20 percent, what ratio do I have?** *(20 for each hundred)* Repeat for other examples.

Mental Math: Finding a Percent of a Number

EXTEND LANGUAGE

Objective Give several fraction-percent benchmarks, and estimate a percent of a whole number using benchmark percents.

ESL Strategies *Use before* **LEARN** ⏱ 10 MIN

Focus on Form ➤ **Imagine you earn $100 a week and want to save about $\frac{1}{3}$ of it. Tell me a math problem you can solve to find how many dollars to save each week.** *(What is about $\frac{1}{3}$ of $100?)* **Sometimes it is easier to change a fraction to a benchmark percent to solve an estimation problem. What benchmark percent is close to $\frac{1}{3}$?** *(30%)* Write "30% of $100" on the board. **Do you want to add, subtract, multiply, or divide the numbers 30% and $100 to find the answer?** *(Multiply)* **How do you know?** *(To find a percent of a number, you multiply the number by the percent.)* Write 30% × $100 below 30% of $100 on the board. **What math symbol replaces the word *of* when you find the percent of a number?** *(Multiplication symbol)*

Have Students ➤ Divide the class into small groups. Write "What is about 12% of 80?" on
Report Back
Orally the board. **Write this problem with math symbols.** *(12% × 80)* Have students question each other about what they wrote and why. Repeat for other problems.

30% of $100
30% × $100

Estimating Percents

ACTIVATE PRIOR KNOWLEDGE/BUILD BACKGROUND; EXTEND LANGUAGE

Objective Give several fraction-percent benchmarks, and estimate a percent of a whole number using benchmark percents.

Materials Index cards

ESL Strategies

Use before **LEARN**   ⏱ 10 MIN

Connect to Prior
Knowledge of
Math

> **What is a benchmark fraction?** *(A fraction that is easy to multiply)* **When do you use benchmark fractions?** *(When you want to estimate)* **What are some useful benchmark fractions?** *($\frac{1}{4}$, $\frac{1}{3}$, $\frac{1}{2}$, $\frac{3}{4}$)* **Write those fractions on the board. Suppose you want to estimate the percent of a number. What kind of percents could you use?** *(Sample answer: Percents that are easy to multiply)* **Let's change the benchmark fractions to percents. What percent is $\frac{1}{4}$?** *(25%)* **$\frac{1}{3}$?** *(33 $\frac{1}{3}$%)* **$\frac{1}{2}$?** *(50%),* **$\frac{3}{4}$?** *(75%)* **Which of these percents is easy to multiply?** *(Sample answer: 50%)* **Why?** *(It is a multiple of 10.)* **How would you use the other percentages to estimate?** *(Round them to the nearest 10.)*

Have Students
Report Back
Orally

> Write percents such as 12%, 53%, or 98% on index cards. Have small groups select 3 cards. **For each card, decide which percent you would use to estimate. Write that percent on the back of the card.** Encourage students to discuss their ideas together before deciding on an answer. Ask each group to select one card and present and explain its answer to the class.

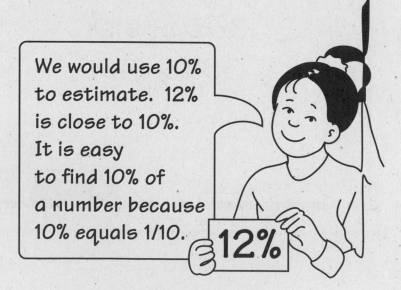

We would use 10% to estimate. 12% is close to 10%. It is easy to find 10% of a number because 10% equals 1/10.

12%

Problem-Solving Applications:
Food

ACCESS CONTENT

Objective Review and apply key concepts, skills, and strategies learned in this and previous chapters.

Language Goal To help students use the language of ratios

Materials *(per pair)* 16 Two-color counters; bag or box

ESL Strategies **Use before** **LEARN** ⏱ 10 MIN

Use Small-Group Interactions ➤ Have a student take a handful of counters and drop them on the desk so that some are red and some are yellow. Suggest that students organize the counters by color. Have one partner ask questions about the 6 kinds of ratios shown and the other partner answer and explain.

What is the ratio of red to yellow counters? *(Sample answer: There are 6 red and 5 yellow counters, so the ratio is 6 to 5.)*

What is the ratio of yellow to red counters? *(Sample answer: There are 5 yellow and 6 red counters, so the ratio is 5 to 6.)*

What is the ratio of red to total counters? *(Sample answer: There are 6 red and 11 total counters, so the ratio is 6 to 11.)*

What is the ratio of total to red counters? *(Sample answer: There are 11 total and 6 red counters, so the ratio is 11 to 6.)*

What is the ratio of yellow to total counters? *(Sample answer: There are 5 yellow and 11 total counters, so the ratio is 5 to 11.)*

What is the ratio of total to yellow counters? *(Sample answer: There are 11 total and 5 yellow counters, so the ratio is 11 to 5.)*

Have students alternate roles and repeat the activity with new counters.

Properties of Equality

EXTEND LANGUAGE; ACCESS CONTENT

USE WITH LESSON **12-1**

Objective Identify and solve equations, and identify variables and the role of variables in equations.

Vocabulary Equation

ESL Strategies   *Use before* **LEARN**   ⏱ 5–10 MIN

Focus on Form ➤   Write "equal" and "equation" on the board. **What does *equal* mean?** *(Having the same value)* **Name some words that have a meaning similar to *equal*.** *(Sample answers: Equivalent, same, alike, identical)* Write 2 + 6 = 11 − 3 on the board. **This is an example of an equation. What do the expressions on both sides of the equal sign have in common?** *(They both equal 8.)* **What is an equation?** *(A mathematical statement in which the two sides are equal)* Underline the first four letters of the word *equation* written on the board so students understand that *equal* is the root of *equation*.

Use Small-Group ➤   Have each student write an equation and a mathematical statement that is not
Interactions   an equation. **Trade papers with another student. Look at the mathematical statements that they have written and circle the equation.** Direct students to check each other's answer. **Why is the other number sentence not an equation?** *(The two sides are not equal.)*

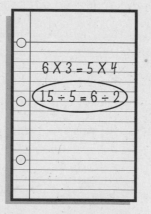

Solving Addition and Subtraction Equations

ACCESS CONTENT

USE WITH LESSON **12-2**

Objective Solve equations involving addition and subtraction.

Materials *(per pair)* paper cup; 10 two-color counters; 2 pieces of paper

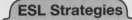
Use Manipulatives ➤ Write $x + 2 = 5$ on the board. **You can model addition equations using cups and counters.** Have student set out the two pieces of paper and explain that each piece represents one side of the equation. **The cup stands for the variable and the counters stand for the numbers. What should you put on the left paper to show the left side of the equation? Explain.** *(Sample answer: I will put a cup to stand for the* x *in the equation and 2 counters to stand for the number 2.)*

What belongs on the other piece of paper to represent the right side of the equation? *(5 counters)* **The equal sign tells you that the number of counters on each piece of paper should be the same. How many counters should you put in the cup to make the sides equal? Explain.** *(3 counters; if I put 3 counters in the cup, I will have 5 counters on each side.)* **What is the value of** x **in the equation? Explain.** *(3; the number of counters in the cup tells me the value of the variable.)*

Have students repeat the activity and explain their solutions to $a + 1 = 3$, $3 + t = 4$, and $6 = z - 2$.

Solving Multiplication and Division Equations

USE WITH LESSON **12-3**

ACTIVATE PRIOR KNOWLEDGE/BUILD BACKGROUND

Objective Solve equations involving multiplication and division.

ESL Strategies | *Use before* **LEARN** | ⏱ 5–10 MIN

Connect to Prior Knowledge of Math ➤ Write $x + 3 = 6$ on the board. **A variable is the unknown value in an equation. It is shown using a letter. What is the variable in this equation?** *(x)* **To solve an equation, we separate the variable so that it is by itself on one side of the equal sign. We do this by using inverse operations. How would you solve the equation on the board?** *(Subtract 3 from both sides of the equation.)* **What is the value of** x? *(3)*

➤ Write $x \times 3 = 6$ below $x + 3 = 6$ on the board. **How are these equations similar and different?** *(They have the same numbers, but the plus sign has been replaced by a multiplication sign in the second equation.)* **What inverse operation would you use to solve this equation?** *(Division)* **Why?** *(Because the left side of the equation is multiplication)* **How would you solve this equation?** *(Divide 3 from both sides of the equation.)* **What is the value of x?** *(2)* Write $x \div 2 = 3$ on the board. **How would you solve this equation?** *(Multiply both sides of the equation by 2.)* **What is the value of x?** *(6)*

Problem-Solving Strategy: Write an Equation

USE WITH LESSON
12-4

ACCESS CONTENT

Objective Write equations for word problems.

Materials *(per student)* Index card with a word problem written on it

ESL Strategies **Use before** **LEARN**   ⏱ 10 MIN

Use ➤
Demonstration

Write "A number plus four equals nine" on the board. **I want to write this problem as an equation with numbers and symbols. The words "A number" tell us that we need to find a value. What would we write to show this unknown amount?** *(A variable)* **Let us use the letter n.** Write "n" below "a number." **What would we write for "plus 4"?** Have a volunteer come up to the board and write $+ 4$ below "plus four." **What would we write for "equals 9"?** Have another volunteer come up to the board and write $= 9$ below "equals 9."

Use Small-Group ➤
Interactions

Divide the class into pairs. Give each student an index card with a word problem that you have written on it, such as "Eleven minus a number is five." **Write this equation with numbers and symbols, then give it to your partner.** Direct the other student to write the equation in words. Have partners compare what was written with the problem on the index card. **Do the word problems match?** If not, have students find the source of the error. Repeat the activity with the other partner's index card.

Understanding Integers

ACTIVATE PRIOR KNOWLEDGE/BUILD BACKGROUND; ACCESS CONTENT

Objective Read, write, compare, and order integers.

ESL Strategies   *Use before* **LEARN**   ⏲ 10 MIN

Connect to Prior Experiences ➤ **If you earned $5, you would have positive $5.** Write +$5 on the board. **How would you show that you owe $5?** Give students time to brainstorm ideas. **You can write "negative $5" to show the amount that you owe.** Write −$5 on the board. **How would you show that the temperature is 12°C above zero?** *(+12°C)* Have a volunteer write his or her answer on the board. **How would you write "12°C below zero?"** *(−12°C)* Have another volunteer write the answer on the board. Repeat for *25 ft above* and *25 ft below* sea level.

Use Graphic Organizers ➤ Draw a large number line on the board from −5 to +5 and label each integer increment. **On the number line, are the positive numbers to the left or right of zero?** *(To the right)* **How do you know?** *(Each of the numbers to the right of zero has a positive sign.)* **Where are the negative numbers?** *(To the left of 0)* **Notice that zero is neither positive nor negative.** Give a direction such as "circle negative 4" and have a volunteer come up to the board and circle the appropriate number. Continue until all of the numbers have been circled. **What number belongs to the right of positive 5?** *(+6)* **Where would you put negative 6?** *(To the left of −5)* **Is positive 1 greater or less than negative 1?** *(Greater)* **How do you know?** *(+1 is to the right of −1.)*

Adding Integers

ACCESS CONTENT

Objective Add integers using a number line.

Materials 11 pieces of paper numbered from 25 to 15, one number to a sheet; tape

ESL Strategies   *Use before* **LEARN**   ⏲ 10 MIN

Use Total Physical Response ➤ Make a number line on the floor by taping down the numbered pieces of paper. Write 3 + 1 on the board. **Where on the number line do we start to solve this problem?** *(On the number 3)* Have a volunteer stand on 3. **How many spaces should (Student) move?** *(1 space)* **Should (Student) move left or right?** *(Right)* **Why?** *(We are adding a positive number.)* Direct the volunteer to move 1 space to the right. **What is the sum of 3 + 1?** *(4)* **How do you know?** *(The student is standing on 4.)* Write the answer on the board.

Write $3 + -1$ on the board. **Where on the number line do we start to solve this problem?** *(On the number 3)* Have a volunteer stand on 3. **How many spaces should (Student) move?** *(1 space)* **Should (Student) move left or right?** *(Left)* **Why?** *(Because we are adding a negative number)* Direct the volunteer to move 1 space to the left. **What is the sum of 3 + −1?** *(2)* **How do you know?** *(The student is standing on 2.)* Write the answer on the board.

Repeat the activity for $1 + -4$. *(−3)* Be sure students understand that the sum of two integers can be negative. Have students also act out and solve $-2 + 3$ and $-1 + -2$. *(1; −3)*

Subtracting Integers

ACCESS CONTENT

Lesson 12-7 icon: USE WITH LESSON 12-7

Objective Subtract integers using a number line.

Materials 11 pieces of paper numbered from −5 to +5, one number to a sheet; tape

ESL Strategies

Use before LEARN

⏱ 10–15 MIN

Use Total ➤
Physical Response

Create a number line from −5 to 5 by taping the cards in order on the floor. Write $1 - 3$ on the board: Have a volunteer model this problem by walking on the number line. **On what number do you start?** *(1)* Have the volunteer stand on "1." **Do you face to the left or the right to model this problem?** *(Left)* **How do you know?** *(Because there is a subtraction sign)* **How many spaces do you walk to the left? Explain.** *(I walk 3 spaces to the left because the second number in the problem is a 3.)* Have the volunteer walk 3 spaces. **What is the answer? How do you know?** *(−2; I am standing on the number −2.)*

Write $1 - (-3)$ on the board. **How is this problem different from the first one?** *(I am subtracting −3 instead of 3.)* Have the volunteer stand on "1." **In the last problem, you faced left to subtract positive 3. Which direction do you want to face to subtract −3?** *(To the right)* Have the volunteer turn and face right.

How many spaces do you walk to the right? *(3 spaces)* Have the volunteer walk 3 spaces. **What is the answer? How do you know?** *(4; I am standing on the number 4.)* Repeat the activity for the problems 2 − 2 and 2 − (−2).

Problem-Solving Skill: Writing to Compare

USE WITH LESSON 12-8

ACCESS CONTENT

Objective Write to explain a pattern.

Materials *(per pair)* Power Polygons

ESL Strategies | *Use before* **LEARN** | ⏱ 10 MIN

Use Manipulatives ➤ Use power polygons to make the pattern circle, circle, square; circle, circle, square; circle, circle, square. **What is the pattern?** *(Circle, circle, square)* **How do you know?** *(The same three shapes repeat three times.)* **What would the next three figures in the pattern be?** *(Circle, circle, square)* Repeat with the pattern circle, square, circle, triangle; circle, square, circle, triangle; circle, square, circle, triangle. Have students explain the pattern and how they know. *(Circle, square, circle, triangle; the same four shapes repeat three times.)*

Use Small-Group Interactions ➤ Arrange students into pairs. Have each partner make a pattern with polygons that repeats at least three times. Have each student then extend his or her partner's pattern with three more figures and describe the pattern.

○ ○ ☐ ○ ○ ☐ ○ ○ ☐

The Coordinate Plane

ACCESS CONTENT; EXTEND LANGUAGE

Objective Identify and graph points on a coordinate plane.

Vocabulary x-axis, y-axis

ESL Strategies | **Use before** LEARN | ⏱ 10 MIN

Use Demonstration ➤ Draw a large coordinate plane on the board or chart paper. Trace and identify the *x*- and *y*-axes. **The *x*-axis is the horizontal or side to side axis. The *y*-axis is the vertical or up and down axis.** Write the ordered pair $(-3, 5)$ on the board. Point to -3. **The *x*-value, -3 in this ordered pair, tells you how many spaces to move left or right from the origin on the *x*-axis. You move left for negative numbers and right for positive numbers.** Point to 5. **The *y*-value, 5 in this ordered pair, tells you how many spaces to move up or down from the origin on the *y*-axis. You move up for positive numbers and down for negative numbers.** Model how to plot $(-3, 5)$ on the graph by tracing from $(0, 0)$ to $(-3, 0)$ with your finger, then from $(-3, 0)$ to $(-3, 5)$. Plot the point.

Have Students Report Back Orally ➤ Have volunteers repeat the demonstration and explain their actions for points such as $(2, -1)$, $(-2, 2)$, and $(-1, -3)$.

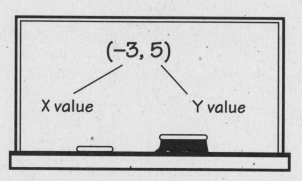

Graphing Equations

ACTIVATE PRIOR KNOWLEDGE/BUILD BACKGROUND

Objective Make a table of *x*- and *y*-values for an equation and then graph the equation.

Vocabulary Table of *x*- and *y*-values

ESL Strategies | **Use before** LEARN | ⏱ 5–10 MIN

Connect to Prior Knowledge of Math ➤ Display a table like the one below. **This is a <u>table of *x*- and *y*-values</u>. Why do you think the table is called that?** (*It is a table with a column of numbers that stand for the variable* x *and a column of numbers that stand for the variable* y.) **How do you think the columns in the table relate to an ordered pair?** (*An ordered pair has an* x- *and a* y-*value. The numbers in the* x *column in the table tell the first number in an ordered pair. The numbers in the* y *column tell the second number.)* **Let us use the numbers in the first row to make an ordered pair.** Add a third column to the table and write an ordered pair template: (__, __). **What is the x-value?** *(2)* Write 2 in the ordered pair. **What is the y-value?** *(1)* Write 1 in the ordered pair. Continue writing ordered pairs for each row of the table, having volunteers identify and write the numbers. Explain that students will learn to use a table to make and graph ordered pairs.

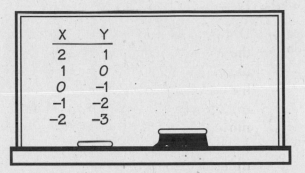

Problem-Solving Applications: Solar System

USE WITH LESSON 12-11

ACCESS CONTENT; EXTEND LANGUAGE

Objective Review and apply key concepts, skills, and strategies learned in this and previous chapters.

Materials *(per group)* 6 colored index cards labeled with different variables such as x and a; 3 cards with − symbols; Number Cards 0–11 (Teaching Tool 8); number cube labeled +, +, +, −, −, −; white index cards

Use Small-Group Interactions ➤ Divide students into groups of 3. Place the variable cards and the number cards face down in separate piles. Have each student take a variable card, a card with an = sign, and 2 number cards. Have each student roll the number cube to select an operation symbol. **Arrange the variable, numbers, and symbols into an equation and write it on an index card.** When students finish writing the equations, have them pass the cards to the right. **Solve the equation and write the solution.** Have students pass the card to the right. **Check the answer. Do you agree?** Give students a chance to correct and discuss any errors. Repeat the activity with new cards and spins.

How did you write the equations? How did you solve the equations? Give students an opportunity to discuss how to solve addition and subtraction equations. *(Sample answer: To solve an addition equation, I subtract the number being added to the variable from both sides. To solve a subtraction equation, I add the number being subtracted from the variable to both sides.)*

Have Students Report Back Orally ➤